The Core Teachings

Buddhist Practice and Progress 1

By
Venerable Master Hsing Yun

Translated by
Pey-Rong Lee and Mu-Tzen Hsu

© 2006 Buddha's Light Publishing

By Venerable Master Hsing Yun
Translated by Fo Guang Shan International Translation Center
Book and cover designed by Dung Trieu
Sculpture of bodhisattva on the cover by Zhang Shude

Published by Buddha's Light Publishing
3456 S. Glenmark Drive
Hacienda Heights, CA 91745, U.S.A.
Tel: (626) 923-5144
Fax: (626) 923-5145
E-mail: itc@blia.org
Website: www.blpusa.com

ISBN-10: 1-932293-24-8
ISBN-13: 978-1-932293-24-1

$\mathcal{A}$cknowledgments

$\mathbf{W}$e received a lot of help from many people and we want to thank them for their efforts in making the publication of this book possible. We especially appreciate Venerable Tzu Jung, the Chief Executive of the Fo Guang Shan International Translation Center (F.G.S.I.T.C.), Venerable Hui Chi, the Abbot of Hsi Lai Temple, Venerable Yi Chao, and Venerable Miao Hsi for their support and leadership; Pey-Rong Lee and Mu-Tzen Hsu for their translation and editing; Venerable Man Jen, Venerable Man Kuang, Scott Hocutt, Marjorie Jacobs, and Derek Hsieh for their assistance in editing and proofreading; Kevin Hsyeh for printing and production; and Dung Trieu for her book and cover design. Portions of this edition were adapted from *Lotus in a Stream*, translated by Tom Graham. Our appreciation also goes out to everyone who has supported this project from its inception to its completion.

TABLE OF CONTENTS

Foreword

In my many travels around the world, I have often been asked the question: "Master, we want to develop our faith in Buddhism, but there are so many books about it. Which book should we read to gain a comprehensive understanding of Buddhism?" Faced with this question, I simply did not know how to answer.

Since the Buddha's words were first written down, the volumes of works based on his teachings have grown astoundingly. The *Tripitaka* alone has more than nine thousand volumes, with several dozen versions in Sanskrit, Pali, Chinese, and Tibetan. Contemporary Buddhist works are similarly daunting in number. Even if one devotes his or her entire life to study them, one may not be able to fully comprehend their essence. Within this immense body of Buddhist literature, finding a single book that is representative of the teachings, and can help ordinary readers gain an integrative understanding of the Buddhist conceptual framework, is truly not an easy task.

I believe that one obstacle to the spread of Buddhism is the sheer quantity and complexity of the Buddhist sutras. Those who are genuinely interested in learning more about Buddhist teachings cannot come to a systematic, organized, and logical understanding of the Dharma from one specific Buddhist work. In contrast, Jews base their faith in the Hebrew Bible while Christians base theirs in the Christian Bible, and both religions have maintained their beliefs through these books without doubt for thousands of years. Muslims have held onto a single Koran, and are even willing to sacrifice their lives for it. On the other hand, due to the daunting volume and complexity of the

Buddhist sutras, it is often difficult for Buddhists to discern which path to take in order to enter the gate of the Dharma. Consequently, some people stop taking steps on the path because of the difficulties they encounter when trying to understand Buddhist concepts, and some, standing outside the gate, dismiss Buddhism as a superstitious religion. Even among longtime devotees and monastics, many are still unable to enter deeply into the Dharma, let alone the readers who are just beginning to study Buddhism.

With this in mind over the years, I have attempted to draft a series of books outlining Buddhist concepts and teachings for the study of Dharma teachers and students at Fo Guang Shan. In this process, efforts were made to prevent them from being either too lengthy or too brief, and to keep the language simple and clear. During the past several years, many people have devoted their time and energy to help review, revise, refine, and translate these works into a series for readers in the West. It is my sincere wish that this work would help readers gain a more comprehensive understanding of the Dharma. I hope this book, and the following books in this series, will be able to realize this wish and benefit all sentient beings.

Hsing Yun
Translated by Derek Hsieh

The Core Teachings

Buddhist Practice and Progress 1

By
Venerable Master Hsing Yun

Translated by
Pey-Rong Lee and Mu-Tzen Hsu

Chapter One

INTRODUCTION

Buddhism originated in India over 2,500 years ago and has spread throughout most of Asia where it has had a tremendous influence on religion, culture, philosophy, and psychology. Within the last century, its popularity has spread to the West, particularly Europe and the United States. It has had an impact on the fields of psychology, philosophy, and neuroscience, disciplines that address the study of the mind and the meaning of existence.

Buddhism is the name given to the practice of the teachings of Sakyamuni Buddha. The Sanskrit word Buddha means the "enlightened one" or "awakened one," and refers to those who have awakened to the Truth. The historical founder of Buddhism was Siddhartha Gautama, who came to be known as Sakyamuni Buddha upon his complete enlightenment. His teachings on seeing the truth of life and awakening to one's true nature are as relevant today as they were in the Buddha's time. However, before we discuss the teachings of the Buddha in depth, let us look at the life of the man whose quest for Truth continues to be the model for those seeking an end to suffering.

THE LIFE OF THE BUDDHA

Before Sakyamuni Buddha was born on earth and became a Buddha for the sake of all sentient beings, he spent countless lives as a bodhisattva. Through eons, the bodhisattva diligently practiced and cultivated, preparing the way to Buddhahood. While still a bodhisattva, he lived in the inner court of Tusita Heaven, the "heaven of the contented ones," where all bodhisattvas who will become Buddhas in their next lifetimes reside. There, he waited for the conditions to be right among sentient beings to appear in our world as the Buddha. When the conditions for rebirth were ripe, the bodhisattva entered the womb of his earthly mother,

Queen Maya.

It was around 500 BCE when the bodhisattva took his final rebirth. The kingdom of Kapilavastu, in present-day southern Nepal, was ruled by the warrior people Sakya. The bodhisattva's father, Suddhodana, was king of the Sakyas, and his mother, Maya, was a princess of Devadaha.

At the end of spring, on the eighth day of the fourth lunar month, a prince was born in Lumbini Garden. It is said that in the first moments after his birth, he took seven steps and, with one hand pointing toward the sky and the other pointing toward the earth, said, "This is my final rebirth in this world. I have appeared in this world to become a Buddha. I will realize the Truth of the universe. I will liberate sentient beings everywhere." The prince was named Siddhartha, which means "accomplishing all."

As was the custom, King Suddhodana summoned the most learned of wise men to foretell his son's destiny. One of the Prince's first visitors was a renowned sage named Asita who predicted that Siddhartha would become a great king of the world if he remained a layperson, or he would become a Buddha who liberates sentient beings if he renounced. On the seventh day after Siddhartha's birth, Queen Maya died. Her sister, Queen Mahaprajapati, lovingly raised the child as her own.

From an early age, it was quite evident that the young Prince was extremely bright and that he excelled in all things. By the time Siddhartha was twelve years old, he was already an expert in the five studies and the four *Vedas*. In addition to his abilities in a wide range of scholarly subjects, he was also an adept warrior who was skilled in the martial arts.

The Prince grew into a young man who was greatly admired for his strength, intelligence, dignity, and beauty. When Siddhartha reached marrying age, King Suddhodana arranged for his son to take a wife. Yasodhara, the beautiful daughter of a Sakya nobleman, was chosen. Many years of wedded happiness followed, and in Siddhartha's twenty-ninth year, his wife gave birth to their son, Rahula.

All this time, King Suddhodana feared that Prince Siddhartha might leave the palace and his royal position. To prevent his son from renouncing, King Suddhodhana sheltered the Prince from the world by building him special palaces and surrounding him with the pleasures of beautiful women, music, wine, and other luxuries. Nevertheless, these worldly pleasures of the palace could not satisfy the feelings of loneliness that had crept into the Prince's heart.

One day, Siddhartha went to tell his father that he wished to travel outside the palace walls to see the kingdom. Hearing this, King Suddhodana immediately ordered that the kingdom be decorated and cleared of anything unpleasant. Furthermore, the elderly, the sick, the ascetics, and corpses were not permitted near the Prince lest they arouse feelings that disturbed his mind.

On his first journey, the Prince and Chandaka, his personal charioteer, saw a frail-looking man who was bent over with age. Siddhartha, shocked by the sight, asked Chandaka about the old man and discovered that old age was a part of the human condition. The Prince was so upset that he asked to be taken back to the palace.

During his second outing, Siddhartha encountered a man who was extremely sick. The Prince again looked to Chandaka for answers. When Chandaka explained that all people fall ill at some point in their lives, the Prince became deeply troubled. Unable to continue onward, the Prince returned to the palace with a heavy heart.

The third time they went driving in the chariot, Siddhartha and Chandaka came upon a funeral procession. The Prince watched as grief-stricken relatives carried a lifeless body through the streets. Some mourners wept softly while others openly wailed in suffering. Distressed by the spectacle, the Prince wished to know why people had to die. Chandaka explained that no one could escape death and everything that is born must one day die. Siddhartha then contemplated all that he had seen, and lamented the realization that life was impermanent.

On a fourth and final journey, Siddhartha and Chandaka encountered an ascetic who walked towards them. The Prince stood up to receive him and asked about his unusual clothing. The man explained that he had renounced the world to seek the Way to liberation from the suffering of old age, illness, and death. After Siddhartha heard these words, his heart filled with joy and his mind gave rise to the thought of taking up the life of a wandering ascetic.

These visions beyond his life of contentment left an indelible impression on Siddhartha. His father noticed the change in him and desperately tried to divert him with more music, beautiful women, feasts, and fine things. However, Siddhartha could not be deterred from his resolve to leave the worldly life behind. One night, not long after the birth of Rahula, the Prince decided to leave the palace and enter the path of cultivation. With one last look at his sleeping wife and infant son, Siddhartha vowed that he would return to see them when he had awakened to the Truth. As everyone slept, he rode away from Kapilavastu with faithful Chandaka by his side.

When they reached a serene forest outside the city, the Prince took off his fine silken clothing and removed his jeweled ornaments. Handing them to Chandaka, Siddhartha told his attendant to return with the horse to Kapilavastu. Then, with his sword, he cut off his long hair and severed all attachments to his old life.

For the next six years, Siddhartha—who now went by his clan name, Gautama—sought out teachers in order to learn how to achieve the Way. Since he had entered the life of an ascetic, Gautama followed the practices of fasting and meditating under extreme conditions of hardship and deprivation. After six years had passed in this way, Gautama was near death. He realized that complete liberation still eluded him, so he abandoned asceticism.

From there, he made his way to Nairanjana where he bathed the filth from his body. As Gautama meditated beneath a banyan tree, he was given an offering of milk rice from the maiden Sujata. When his strength returned, he traveled to Bodhgaya where he seated himself on a diamond throne under a *bodhi* tree and began to meditate. He swore that he would not stir from his seat, even at the cost of his life, until he had liberated himself from the cycle of birth and death and attained enlightenment.

Sitting in meditation, Gautama conquered the demons of his mind–greed, anger, and ignorance–as well as *Mara*, the king of the demons. After defeating *Mara*, Gautama entered the state of *samadhi*. Through this deep contemplation, he first saw all of his countless past lives. Then, he realized the non-duality of birth and death. With his wisdom-eye, he saw sentient beings within the six realms of existence suffering endlessly from karmic cause and effect. In the third realization, he came to understand the Law of Dependent Origination. Even after he realized the Truth of the universe, Gautama continued to meditate and contemplate under the *bodhi* tree for twenty-one days.

At the first light of dawn, Gautama finally awakened to the root of suffering–ignorance. Thus, he found the way leading to the cessation of this suffering. Forty-nine days after he had made his vow, on the eighth day of the twelfth lunar month under a night sky filled with stars, Gautama attained complete enlightenment on the diamond throne. He was thirty-five years old. From this moment forth, he was known as Sakyamuni Buddha–the sage of the Sakyas.

After his enlightenment, the Buddha spent forty-five years teaching the Dharma. At the age of eighty, on the fifteenth day of the second lunar month, under a pair of *sala* trees, the Buddha entered *parinirvana.* The legacy he left his disciples was profound, for the Buddha had dedicated his earthly life to teaching others the Four Noble Truths, dependent origination, cause and effect, karma, the Three Dharma Seals, emptiness, the Noble Eightfold Path, the Five Precepts, the six perfections, and the Middle Way. Ever since Sakyamuni Buddha transmitted the Dharma to his disciples, count-less sentient beings through the centuries have heard the teachings, cultivated the Path, and attained enlightenment.

Chapter Two

HOW TO STUDY BUDDHISM

When the Buddha taught the Dharma, he gave the world an inexhaustible gift: the ability to find true freedom. The Dharma is a mirror that reflects the truths within us and shows us how to free ourselves from our own delusions. These truths are the same truths that govern the universe. As we examine our mind in the mirror of the Buddha's teachings, we will discover that the wisdom we have always possessed is gradually awakening.

The value of learning the Dharma is not something that can be easily measured. The first step we must take when we enter the gate of the Dharma is to look at ourselves. We must decide that we want to change, that we want to learn, and that we will really try to apply the Buddha's teachings in our daily lives. The moment we embrace the Dharma, our lives will begin to change. It is like a light that will forever illuminate the darkness.

The process of learning the Dharma is the most exciting and wonderful kind of self-discovery in the world. In the sections below, I will try to explain how to approach the Dharma and practice it in our lives.

THE FOUR RELIANCES

The truths that the Buddha taught are fundamental truths, which mean that they are true everywhere and at all times. As Buddhist practitioners searching for the Dharma, we must rely on four guidelines to keep us on the right path. These Four Reliances are to: rely on the Dharma, not on people; rely on wisdom, not on knowledge; rely on the meaning, not on the words; and rely on the definitive meaning, not on the provisional one.

Rely on the Dharma, Not on People. To rely on the Dharma is to rely on the Truth regardless of what we do. We cannot rely on people because everyone has different perceptions and interpretations. People are subject to birth, aging, sickness, and death, but the Dharma has never changed since beginningless time. So in seeking the Way, we must always rely on the Dharma and not on people.

Although there are people who can instruct us and help us along the Path, we still must experience and understand it for ourselves in order to truly make it our own. When learning from others, we should examine everything under the lens of our own introspection. In a famous Chan story, a student once asked Chan Master Zhaozhou (778-897) how to learn the Dharma so he could attain the Way. Master Zhaozhou stood up and said, "I am going to go take a piss now. Ah! Even trivial matters such as taking a piss need to be done by oneself."

Sakyamuni Buddha once said that we should rely on ourselves and rely on the Dharma, not on others. This is to say that we should always believe in ourselves, rely on ourselves, believe in the Truth, and rely on the Truth. Therefore, we should listen to the teachings of the Buddha and the instructions of our teachers, but if we truly wish to gain wisdom we still must rely on ourselves to experience the Truth.

Rely on Wisdom, Not on Knowledge. What is the difference between wisdom and knowledge? Wisdom is the Truth that already lies within us. Knowledge is what we have gained through our experiences in the outside world.

So why must we rely on wisdom and not on knowledge? The knowledge that we acquire through our six organs (eyes, ears, nose, tongue, body, and consciousness) is constantly shifting with the changes of phenomena. This is why knowledge is not complete enough. On the other hand, wisdom is like the big round mirror of our true nature. When we use this mirror to look at all the phenomena of the universe, it will reflect things as they really are. As we walk down the path of cultivation, if we can see the reality of all things with our wisdom and not discriminate based on our knowledge, we will not be deluded by the illusions of the world.

Rely on Meaning, Not on Words. We often gain knowledge and realize the truth through the medium of language and words. While there are many different languages throughout the world, the Truth that they express is essentially the same. By realizing this, we will grasp the essential meaning of all things instead of being mired in the words. If we are too attached to the language and words, what we end up with is superficial understanding without comprehending the real meaning.

The unusual behavior of Chan masters was calculated to open our minds to this point. In a famous Chan *gongan* (also known in Japanese as *koan*), a Chan master said, "Today, if I could still see Sakyamuni Buddha speak on the Dharma, I'd beat him to death with a stick and feed him to the dogs!" Another example is, "What doctrine of the *Tripitaka*? Bring it here. I'll use it as a rag!" The Chan master's wild words may seem to slander the Buddha and the Dharma, but in fact, he wants us to transcend the attachment to language and words, and realize the Truth beyond them.

Rely on Definitive Meaning, Not on Provisional Meaning. When we say, "rely on the definitive meaning," this means that we rely on the ultimate Truth and not on the various methods of teaching. Buddhism has divided into different traditions in order to teach the Dharma to as many sentient beings as possible. Within these traditions, many different schools have been established based on various methods of cultivation.

The various methods of cultivating the Dharma that the Buddha taught us are all "skillful means" or "expedient means" because they are tailored to the different needs and capacities of sentient beings. However, we cannot consider these skillful means as the ultimate way to learn the Dharma since they are provisional, and change with the person and the conditions. According to the Buddha, the ultimate way is to follow the definitive meaning of the Dharma, which is in accord with the Buddha mind.

FOUR STATES OF MIND FOR STUDYING THE DHARMA

What state of mind should Buddhist practitioners have when they study the Dharma? To be able to receive the teachings, we must possess a mind with faith, a mind that questions, a mind of awakening, and finally, no-mind.

Use Faith to Study the Dharma. The object of studying Buddhism is to purify and settle our body and mind, elevate our character, open up our world, and give us direction in our lives. Buddhism can help us discover that we are the "master" of our mind. On this path to self-discovery, faith plays an important role.

Dr. Sun Yat-sen (1866-1925), regarded as the Father of the Republic of China, once said, "Faith is strength." The *Treatise on the Perfection of Great Wisdom* says, "The Dharma is like the great ocean. Only with faith can we enter it." The *Flower Ornament Sutra* says, "Faith is the origin of the Way and the mother of all virtues. It nourishes all good roots."

There is a story in Buddhism that illustrates how faith gives us strength. In the countryside, there was a little old lady who wished to learn the Dharma. Unfortunately, there was no one around to teach her. One day, a layman who did not have a good grasp of Buddhism came to this village. When he saw how much the little old lady wanted to learn the Dharma, he said, "I know a Buddhist *mantra* I can teach to you. It is, 'Om Mani Padme Hum.'" However, the layman mispronounced the word "Hum," saying "Um" instead.

The old lady did not know any better, so every day, she chanted "Om Mani Padme Um." Each time she chanted the *mantra*, she would pick up a bean and place it in a bowl. After many years of chanting in this way, she did not need to pick up the beans anymore. Whenever she chanted "Om Mani Padme Um" in her mind, the beans would jump into the bowl on their own.

Several years later, a monastic came to the village. Hearing the old lady chant "Om Mani Padme Um," he went to tell her that she had been chanting the mantra incorrectly. When the old lady heard this, she thought, "Oh dear! I've chanted it wrong all these years." Thereafter, she corrected herself, but the beans no longer jumped into the bowl by themselves.

Whether we say "Hum" or "Um" is unimportant; as long as we have faith, this faith will give us strength. The importance of faith is like the roots of a tree. If we do not have faith, we cannot accomplish anything, for faith gives rise to strength. As Buddhist practitioners, we should have faith and use this sincere mind of faith to study the Dharma.

Use Questioning to Study the Dharma. What state of mind should Buddhist practitioners approach the Dharma with? Perhaps many of you have doubts and questions? The Buddha taught that we should study the Dharma with a questioning mind. This is how Buddhism is different from other religions, for aside from emphasizing faith, it also tells us to doubt. In the Chan School of Buddhism, practitioners are encouraged to give rise to the mind that doubts and asks questions. This is why they say in the Chan School, "Small doubts lead to small awakenings. Great doubts lead to great awakenings. No doubts lead to no awakening."

The Dharma is like a great bell. If you tap it gently it will ring softly. If you strike it hard it will resound loudly. However, if you do not strike it at all, it will not ring. We must have questions in order to gain answers. In fact, the content of the Buddhist sutras is made up of the disciples' questions and the Buddha's answers.

Chan Buddhism instructs practitioners to question and investigate. This method is called *huatou*, which literally means "speech head," or essential words. For hundreds of years, Chan masters have used this method to achieve awakening. As a result, there are many records of the exchanges between Chan masters and their students. They are so profound and difficult that the average person cannot understand, let alone answer. For example, in the Chan meditation hall, masters ask questions such as: "What was my original face before my parents gave birth to me?" "What is the great meaning of Bodhidharma coming to the West?" "Who is reciting the Buddha's name?" These Chan questions require us to bring forth our doubts so that we can gain wisdom and awaken to the truth.

Use the Awakened Mind to Study the Dharma. People go to school to gain knowledge and they study the Dharma to seek enlightenment. Awakening is not the process of accumulating knowledge; it is the moment of sudden realization. It is when we think, "Ah ha! I understand." How then, do we reach the state of awakening?

There was a young student who went to ask a Chan master, "I just came to the monastery and do not understand anything. Master, please instruct me on how to enter the Way?"

The Chan master replied, "Do you hear the birds singing in the tree? The crickets chirping? Can you see the water flowing in the stream? The flowers blooming?"

The young student replied, "Yes!"

Then the Chan master told him, "The Way is entered from all these things."

We can see that the Dharma is not mysterious, nor is it separate from our lives. It is always a part of the world around us. When we "understand" the sound of the flowing water, that is the sound of the Buddha's voice. When we see the blooming flowers, it is the pure Dharma-body of the Buddha. When we awaken to the Truth, everything we do is the Way. We do not need to go far to seek the Way for it is in our lives and in our mind.

There is another Chan *gongan* that demonstrates this point. When Chan Master Longtan (dates of birth and death unknown) was still a novice, he went to study under Master Tianhuang (748-807). Year after year passed, but Chan Master Tianhuang never instructed him in the Dharma. After a long time, Longtan became frustrated and went to bid farewell to Chan Master Tianhuang. Surprised by this, Tianhuang said to him, "Oh! Where are you going?"

Chan Master Longtan said, "I am going elsewhere to seek the Dharma."

Chan Master Tianhuang replied, "There is the Dharma right here. Why do you need to go somewhere else to study?"

Longtan replied, "I've been here for a long time. How come I've never heard you speak the Dharma to me?"

Chan Master Tianhuang replied, "When you bring me tea, I use my hands to take it from you. When you bring me food, I use my mouth to eat it. When you bow to me, I nod to you. When have I not spoken the Dharma to you?" After he heard this, Longtan bowed his head and began to think.

Tianhuang then said, "Don't think. Once you think, you've gone astray. You need to experience and directly bear responsibility."

With these words, Longtan suddenly had a great awakening.

Actually, the Dharma is in our every action, and Chan is in every flower, tree, and stone. We usually do not realize the Dharma is in our mind, so we look for it outside of ourselves. Yet, the more we seek, the farther away we get from the Way. The Dharma teaches us that we must always seek within. If we can do this, the Way will become very close to us.

Use No-Mind to Study the Dharma. No-mind is the true mind; it is the mind that does not differentiate. No-mind also transcends the duality of having and not having. When studying the Dharma, we cannot approach it with a differentiating mind because differentiations are based on knowledge that is constantly changing. On the other hand, the non-differentiating mind is a kind of wisdom. Only with this mind of wisdom can we deeply penetrate the truths of the Dharma.

In the past, someone asked a Chan master, "Master, you usually meditate for a very long time. May I ask: do you enter *samadhi* with mind or no-mind?"

The Chan master answered, "When I enter *samadhi*, it is

neither with mind nor with no-mind. I enter it with the mind that is beyond all duality."

When we talk about this mind that transcends duality, it does not mean that we do not have any concept of right and wrong, or good and bad. In fact, we should have these concepts. However, in dealing with worldly affairs and dualities, we need to face them with the non-differentiating mind, the mind of wisdom.

Once a student asked Chan Master Guishan (771-853), "What is the Way?"

Chan Master Guishan replied, "No-mind is the Way."

The student said, "I don't know how!"

Guishan replied, "Go find someone who knows how."

The student said, "Who knows how?"

The master said, "It is not someone else. It is yourself!"

No-mind allows us to see the world as it really is, not as our differentiating mind tells us it is. By applying no-mind to the world around us, we will gain the clarity to see the Buddha in everything and our Buddha nature within.

Chapter Three

DEPENDENT ORIGINATION

Sitting on the diamond throne underneath the *bodhi* tree, the Buddha gazed up at the stars and attained enlightenment. The Truth that he awakened to was the universal truth of dependent origination, one of the central teachings in Buddhism. Dependent origination is also the most significant characteristic that distinguishes Buddhism from other philosophies and religions.

What is dependent origination? "Dependent origination" means that all phenomena do not arise from nothing, they cannot exist by themselves, and the right conditions must come together before these phenomena can arise and come into existence. The *Commentary on the Surangama Sutra* states, "The simplest to the most profound teachings say that all phenomena do not exist outside of causes and conditions," and the Buddhist sutras also say, "All phenomena arise from causes and conditions."

DEPENDENT ORIGINATION AND
CAUSES AND CONDITIONS

All phenomena in the world come into being because of causes and conditions. Without them, no phenomena would appear in this world and no phenomena could exist in this world.

Stated simply like this, the truth of dependent origination may seem obvious or trivial, yet it has far-reaching consequences, for it means that nothing has an independent existence of its own. There is no "self" that exists separately from others. It also means that there is no absolute phenomenon anywhere in the universe. Since all phenomena are interdependent, if the causes and conditions that produce or sustain a phenomenon are removed, that phenomenon will cease to exist.

The Buddha said, "All phenomena arise from causes and conditions. All phenomena disappear due to causes and conditions." But what are they? Where do they come from? Causes and conditions themselves are phenomena, and they arise themselves from other causes and conditions.

The Buddha called some phenomena causes and others conditions to help us understand the way in which phenomena arise and cease. The words "cause" and "condition" have meaning only in relation to each other. What is a cause here may be seen as a phenomenon there or as a condition somewhere else. It all depends on the angle from which we observe it.

Cause and condition are the two basic factors that produce or underlie each and every phenomenon in the universe. The primary condition, which is more powerful, is known as the "cause" and the secondary condition is simply called the "condition." For example, a seed that is planted in the soil needs water, fertilizer, air, and sunlight to grow. The seed is the cause while the soil, water, fertilizer, air, and sunlight are the conditions. Only when all of the right causes and conditions are present, can there be a result or an effect. Without a cause, there could be no effect. With a cause but no conditions, there would also be no effect. When both the causes and conditions come together, that will produce an effect.

Dependent origination is not something invented by the Buddha. It is a universal principle underlying all phenomena in the universe. When the Buddha became enlightened, he "merely" awakened to this principle. After his enlightenment, the Buddha taught others what he had come to understand. He taught that if we contemplate the concept of causes and conditions from the perspective of sentient beings trapped within the cycle of birth and death, we should be able to see that our lives have not been created by some god that stands outside of the universe, but rather that our lives are the result of a complex interaction of causes and conditions.

DEPENDENT ORIGINATION AND CAUSE AND EFFECT

In the section above, we moved toward an understanding of dependent origination by focusing on the causes and conditions that produce all phenomena in the universe. In this section, we will deepen our understanding of dependent origination by focusing on the interactions of cause and effect. The Law of Cause and Effect is the fundamental principle that underlies all phenomena. Every phenomenon is caused by other phenomena and every phenomenon also produces effects.

The *Connected Discourses of the Buddha* says, "This exists, therefore, that exists. This arises, therefore, that arises. This is absent, therefore, that is absent. This is extinguished, therefore, that is extinguished."

The "this" and "that" of the above quotation refer to cause and effect. This quote implies that neither cause nor effect has an independent nature. They both exist together in a state of dynamic interaction. Without one, the other could not be. Just as the words "cause" and "condition" are relative terms, so are the words "cause" and "effect." In reality, this universe is an extremely complicated web of dynamically and intricately interrelated phenomena. The Buddha used the words "cause," "condition," "effect," and "result" to help us understand some of the general features of this dynamically interactive web. It is important for each one of us to try to understand this universe because this is where we live. We are an intrinsic part of it, and what we think about it has great influence both on ourselves and on other sentient beings.

There are six principles that are crucial to our understanding of the Law of Cause and Effect. They are: effects arise from causes, temporary appearances depend on causes and conditions, events depend on the Law of Cause and Effect, many come from one, existence relies on emptiness, and a Buddha comes from a human being. The following sections will discuss each of these basic concepts in order. By considering the meaning and implications of each of these basic ideas, we will arrive at a better understanding of dependent origination.

Effects Arise from Causes. Dependent origination first depends on the presence of a cause and then on the right conditions, before the result or effect can manifest. If there is no cause, there can be no effect. If there is a cause, but conditions are not right, then there also will be no effect. The cause is the primary and internal requirement for the arising of phenomena, and the direct force for producing the effect. The conditions are the external requirements that help the cause to produce an effect, and are considered to be an indirect force for creating the effect.

For example, all human beings have the seed (or cause) of Buddhahood within them. But if this seed is not surrounded by good conditions (i.e. studying the Dharma, practicing the precepts, and so forth), then that seed will not likely grow into a healthy plant. Similarly, a person who has a seed of anger inside him may be able to control that anger for many years. However, if the conditions are right, he may suddenly explode seemingly without reason. Therefore, the cause is the primary requirement for any effect while conditions are secondary requirements.

All phenomena in the universe are governed by causes and conditions. Away from this kind of relationship, there is absolutely no substantial existence of phenomena. All phenomena exist due to their own causes and conditions.

Temporary Appearances Depend on Causes and Conditions. From the principle "effects arise from causes," we know that all phenomena do not arise by themselves; they rely on circumstances to manifest. These circumstances refer to causes and conditions. It can be said that "all phenomena arise from causes and conditions; all phenomena extinguish due to causes and conditions." Therefore, all phenomena in the world are "temporary appearances" that result from the combination of causes and conditions, and the forms of phenomena themselves have no substantial existence. Since they have no substantial existence, phenomena appear following the arising of conditions, and disappear following the ceasing of conditions. This is what is meant by, "everything comes from dependent origination, and everything's nature is empty."

Events Depend on the Law of Cause and Effect. The arising of phenomena, appearances, and events require causes and conditions, but it also underlies the universal principle, which is the Law of Cause and Effect. If you plant a pumpkin seed, you will not reap a tomato. Causes of one type produce effects that are consistent with that type. This is a certain truth. Against this law, no event can occur.

Many Come from One. To the average person, "one" is "one," and "many" is "many." But in Buddhism, "one" is "many" and "many" is "one," and furthermore, "many" come from "one." Most people do not look at the world in this way; accordingly, they do not reap the benefits of Buddhist practice. They do not understand the potential that lies within things and especially within the human mind. Just as one seed may grow into a tree that produces many fruit, many fruit also comes from just one seed. Likewise, one small act of kindness may create many ripples that change the world for the better, and one small act of intentional cruelty may cause many destructive results that could last for a long time.

Existence Relies on Emptiness. The principles we have been discussing, such as "effects arise from causes" or "events depend on the Law of Cause and Effect," exist. In Buddhism, it is said that existence relies on emptiness, which means that all phenomena have no "independent" nature. Since all things are interconnected, not one of them can be said to have a permanent, substantial existence. Ultimately, the nature of all things is "empty"; their existence relies on "emptiness."

An example that is commonly used to explain this point is that of the wooden table. A table comes from a tree, and the tree depends on the conditions of soil, water, and sunshine to grow. Even though a table appears have some substantial existence, it actually relies on many different conditions coming together to give it a temporary appearance. Aside from the external conditions that gave rise to the tree, someone had to cut the tree, move it, make the table, and put it in your room. As soon as we begin to investigate the causes and conditions on which the table depends for its existence, we find that ultimately there is no "table nature." Rather, there is only an endlessly complex web of interconnectedness, impermanence, and change. If even one element is removed from that web, there might not be a table at all.

None of this says that the table does not exist. It means that the nature of a table is empty. If the nature of phenomena were not empty, there would be no way to demonstrate the value and function of all things. This function is known as "the function of emptiness." The value and function of a table belongs to conventional reality. The "emptiness" of the table belongs to ultimate reality.

Understanding emptiness requires that we understand the impermanence and interconnectedness of all things. When we understand that all things are impermanent and interconnected, then we can understand that not one of them has its own substantial existence.

The great Buddhist philosopher, Nagarjuna, said, "Because there is emptiness, all dharmas exist. Without emptiness, all dharmas could not be." This is to say, emptiness is what all things rely on. If there were no emptiness, myriad things would not be able to exist. Therefore, the existence of all things must rely on emptiness to come into being.

A Buddha Comes from a Human Being. When Sakyamuni Buddha became enlightened, he said, "All sentient beings in the universe have the wisdom and virtue of a Tathagata, but because of delusions and attachments, they cannot awaken." The Buddha said time and again that all of us have Buddha nature and that anyone who works long and hard enough at purifying his or her mind will eventually attain Buddhahood. Our attachments are like dark clouds that conceal the brightness of the moon and like mud that obscures a pond's clear water.

In our study of Buddhism, we must understand the truth of the cycle of birth and death and the truth that "This is absent, therefore, that is absent. This is extinguished, therefore, that is extinguished" to end our ignorance and reveal our Buddha nature. We will then attain the state of non-duality, the state without the limitations of space and time, and the state without birth and death. This is the state of enlightenment. Now, we can see that "a Buddha is an enlightened sentient being and sentient beings are yet to be enlightened Buddhas." The *Sutra on the Principles of the Six Perfections* says, "All sentient beings enter into the wisdom of the Buddha by purifying their minds. The nature of a Buddha is no different from that of any other sentient being." In addition to these principles, I will discuss some basic characteristics of the Law of Cause and Effect in the following section.

In the Law of Cause and Effect, there is no first cause and there is no last effect. This is because the present cause contains many previous causes. By this assumption, there is no beginning. Likewise, after the present effect, more effects will follow. By this assumption, there is no end.

Cause and effect are related, but the roles they play are not absolute. Causes produce effects, but those effects in turn produce other effects, and in doing so, become causes. Causes and effects are really interlocking parts of an endless chain of events. Seen from one angle, a cause is a cause. Seen from another angle, it becomes an effect.

Cause and effect pervades the three times periods of past, present, and future. It is sometimes hard for us to understand and accept that our intentional behavior produces effects. We cannot hide anywhere from the consequence of our own actions. We may wait ten million years, but one day, when the conditions are right, the effects of our behavior will manifest.

Cause and effect are two sides of the same coin. Every cause contains effects just as every effect contains a cause. If you

plant a bean, you will not harvest a melon. If you intentionally perform a bad deed, you will not reap a reward.

FOUR KINDS OF CONDITIONS
IN DEPENDENT ORIGINATION

For cause and effect to work, there must be right conditions. Dependent origination is the interplay between cause, effect,
and conditions. Although causes are primary, conditions are very
important in this process. There are four basic kinds of conditions
that are related to our discussion of dependent origination. They
are as follows:

1. The causal condition. The causal condition refers to the
internal cause that directly produces the effect. For example,
the seed that produces a seedling is considered to be a causal
condition of that seed.
2. Conditions without intervals. Conditions without intervals
are also called "successive conditions." This refers to the cause
of a thought that gives rise to the next thought in activities of
the mind. This activity is continuous from moment to moment,
so these conditions are also successive and have no intervals.
3. Conditional conditions. Conditional conditions are all external conditions that have bearing on the mind. For example, the
conditional condition of the eye consciousness is color, of the
ear consciousness is sound, and of the mind consciousness is
the phenomena of the past, present, and future.
4. Advancing conditions. All conditions that help or do not hin-
der the arising of phenomena are called advancing conditions.

The four kinds of conditions discussed above can also be
thought of as being either "direct conditions" or "indirect conditions." All causal conditions are considered to be conditions that
operate directly on phenomenon, while the three other kinds of
conditions are considered to operate indirectly.

Further insight into the four kinds of conditions is that

material phenomena only require causal conditions and advancing conditions to function. Phenomena of the mind, in contrast, require all four conditions to operate.

DEPENDENT ORIGINATION AND HUMAN LIFE

Dependent origination shows us the relationship among arising, extinguishing, and changing of phenomena as well as the origin of human suffering. If we ignore or discount the fact that all things are impermanent and change due to causes and conditions, we are setting ourselves up to suffer. Whenever we ignore the reality of dependent origination and are attached to the delusion of permanence, we bring suffering onto ourselves. In contrast, when we are mindful of the forces that affect the phenomenal world, we prepare ourselves to deal with them in a positive and productive manner. If we understand that many are born from one and that all conditions are caused, then we will understand how to bring about good conditions in our own lives and the world in general.

A true understanding of dependent origination brings joy to the mind because dependent origination teaches us that our futures lie in our own hands. Future conditions depend on causal seeds that we plant today. Liberation is achieved through understanding this truth and using it for the betterment of all sentient beings. A clear understanding of dependent origination strengthens our mind because this truth teaches us how to understand what is most valuable in life and how to turn negative circumstances into positive ones.

Dependent origination teaches us that nothing in the world is permanent and explains why this is so. To understand dependent origination is to understand that all phenomena are conditioned by other phenomena and that all of them "rely on emptiness." Nothing has a substantial existence, including us. Ultimately, we too are empty. Clear understanding of this truth leads to liberation in a reality that lies beyond greed, anger, ignorance, attachment, suffering, and all delusions of duality.

Frequent contemplation of dependent origination can

inspire us to be grateful for the things we have and the world we live in. It can teach us how to flow with life in a way that benefits both others and ourselves. Dependent origination gives us hope as it shows us how to understand the deepest meaning of life. The *Rice Stalk Sutra* says, "To see dependent origination is to see the Dharma. To see the Dharma is to see the Buddha."

Chapter Four

THE FOUR NOBLE TRUTHS

When Sakyamuni Buddha became enlightened, he saw that the entire phenomenal universe functions in accordance with the truth of dependent origination. When he decided to teach others what he had realized, the Buddha knew that if he explained dependent origination directly to them, it would be difficult for them to understand, and it might even cause them to become afraid. For this reason, in his first teachings, the Buddha taught the Four Noble Truths instead of the truth of dependent origination. The first time the Buddha taught is called the "First Turning of the Dharma Wheel."

The Four Noble Truths, dependent origination, and the Three Dharma Seals are the most basic principles of Buddhist doctrine. Although they go by different names, their meanings are all interrelated. The Four Noble Truths simply turn the focus of dependent origination directly onto human life. For this reason, they seem more relevant to human beings and easier to understand.

The Four Noble Truths are: the truth of suffering, the truth of the causes of suffering, the truth of the cessation of suffering, and the truth of the path leading to the cessation of suffering. The word "suffering" in this definition is a standard English translation of the Sanskrit word *dukkha*, which literally means "unsatisfactory."

The word "noble" means "righteousness." According to the sutras, "The noble are also righteous, and they apply righteousness in all matters. This is what is called 'noble.'" The meaning of the word "truth" in the Four Noble Truths is explained in the *Commentary on the Stages of Yogacara Practitioners*: "From the truth of suffering to the truth of the path leading to the cessation of suffering, it is all true, not upside down. Thus, it is called 'truth.'" It also says, "Only those who are noble can understand these truths and contemplate them. Those who are ignorant can neither understand them nor contemplate them. Thus, these truths are called 'noble truths.'" When we can fully understand the Four Noble Truths, we are noble. The *Commentary on the Treatise of the Middle Way* says, "The Four Noble Truths are the root of ignorance and enlightenment. In the state of ignorance, you will be trapped within the chaos of the six realms. In the state of awakening, you will become a sage of the three vehicles."

The *Sutra of the Teachings Bequeathed by the Buddha* says, "The moon may become hot and the sun may grow cold, but the Four Noble Truths will never change."

The Four Noble Truths stand at the core of all life. They explain all phenomena in the universe, and they teach us how to achieve liberation from all delusions.

Understanding the Four Noble Truths depends on wisdom. The first truth is: life is full of suffering. The second truth says that suffering is caused by our attachments to delusion. The third truth says that enlightenment or complete liberation from all suffering is possible. The fourth truth teaches us how to become enlightened.

The first two of the Four Noble Truths have a cause and effect relationship with each other. The First Noble Truth is the effect and the second is its cause. The second two of the Four Noble Truths also have a cause and effect relationship with each other. The Third Noble Truth is an effect that is caused by the Fourth Noble Truth.

At first glance, you might wonder why the Buddha placed the Four Noble Truths in the order he did. It seems more logical to place the second and fourth truths, which are both causes, before the first and the third truths, which are both effects. The Buddha chose to use a different order because he wanted to teach them in the most effective way possible. Since it is easier for most people to grasp the effect and then come to understand its causes, the Buddha placed the truth of suffering first. Then he explained the causes of suffering. Once people understand the first two Noble Truths, they naturally want to liberate themselves from their suffering. To help us understand how to achieve liberation, the Buddha taught the Third Noble Truth, which is the cessation of suffering. Then he taught the Fourth Noble Truth, which is the way that leads to the cessation of suffering.

Central to all of the Buddha's teachings is the immense compassion he showed in crafting explanations that are designed to be understandable to everyone. Dependent origination and the Four Noble Truths are very profound truths. Anyone who fully studies these doctrines will eventually realize how compassionate and wise the Buddha was in being able to teach them so clearly.

THE FIRST NOBLE TRUTH

Suffering is the state in which the body and mind are driven by afflictions. The truth of suffering describes how the reality of life is full of suffering. The Buddha saw with perfect clarity that each one of us cannot escape from this reality, and that it is not possible for a human being to achieve complete satisfaction in this world. Buddhist sutras show suffering in many different ways. In the following sections, I will discuss the three most basic classifications of suffering as described in the sutras.

The Two Sufferings. The "two sufferings" are internal sufferings and external sufferings. This is the most basic classification of suffering mentioned in the Buddhist sutras. It is the most basic way to understand suffering. Internal sufferings are all of those sufferings that we usually think of as being part of ourselves. These include physical pain, anxiety, fear, jealousy, suspicion, anger, and so forth. External sufferings are all of those sufferings that seem to come from the outside. These include wind, rain, cold, heat, drought, wild animals, natural disasters, wars, criminals, etc. None of us can avoid either of these kinds of suffering.

The Three Sufferings. The "three sufferings" focus more on the quality of suffering rather than on its origin or type. The first of the three sufferings is suffering within suffering, the suffering that comes from just being alive as well as the conditions of hunger, disease, wind and rain, labor, hot and cold, and casualties of war. The second is the suffering of deterioration. The suffering of deterioration refers to the breakdown of the state of happiness. This is caused by the passage of time, or is broken down by external conditions leading to the suffering of the body and mind. For example, objects break, people die, and everything ages and declines. Even the best of times must all come to an end. The third suffering is the suffering of process. The suffering of process is that which comes from living in a world where phenomena are constantly changing. In our world, we have little or no control over our lives. We experience anxiety, fear, and helplessness as we watch everything change from day to day.

The Eight Sufferings. The "eight sufferings" are a more detailed description of the suffering that all sentient beings must endure. The eight sufferings are grouped according to what they describe. The first is the suffering of birth. Following many dangerous months in our mother's womb, we at last experience the pain and fear of birth. After that, anything can happen. We are like prisoners in our bodies and of the worlds into which we are born.

The second is the suffering of aging. If we are fortunate enough not to die when we are still young, we will have to face the suffering of growing old and of watching our body and mind decline.

The third is the suffering of illness. When we are sick, we might suffer from aches and pains, cuts and bruises, poor digestion, organ failure, paralysis, or respiratory problems. All of us at some time must suffer from the pain of illness.

The fourth is the suffering of death. Even if our lives are somehow perfect, we still will die. If death is not sudden and frightening, then it is too often slow and painful. Especially at the moment of death, when the body and mind begin to decompose, there is extreme suffering. This is what is meant by the suffering of death.

The fifth is the suffering of separation from loved ones. It stems from our strong attachments. Sometimes we lose the ones we love, and sometimes they do not love us in return. We suffer because we cannot always be with the people we love.

The sixth is the suffering of encountering objects of hate. When we have to deal with people we really dislike, we suffer. For example, at work we might dislike our boss, or we cannot tolerate a particular coworker. However, when we are forced to interact with them, we suffer.

The seventh is the suffering of not getting what we want. As human beings, we have attachments. When we encounter objects of our desire and we doggedly pursue them, but we still cannot obtain them, we suffer.

The eighth is the suffering of the blaze of the five aggregates, which are the five components of existence: form, feeling, perception, mental formation, and consciousness. They are the "building blocks" of a sentient being, and the means through which all suffering occurs. When the five aggregates come together, they become the unlimited fuel source that produces pain and suffering life after life after life.

The Basic Causes of Suffering. In the above sections, we have discussed some of the basic ways Buddhists understand human life as being mired in suffering. In the following sections, we will look more deeply into the subject of suffering as we delineate some of its most basic causes.

The self is not in harmony with the material world. We are constantly struggling to find comfort in this world. When our houses are too small and there are too many people, we will feel discomfort. When our desk is too high or too low, the lamp is too bright or too dim, we may find it difficult to study with ease. The material world does not revolve around us in just the way we would like, so we suffer.

The self is not in harmony with other people. All too often we cannot be with the people we want to be with, but are forced to spend time with people who are difficult for us to get along with. Sometimes, we are even forced to spend time with people who openly dislike us.

The self is not in harmony with the body. The body is born, grows old, gets sick, and dies. The "self" has little or no control over this process.

The self and the mind are not in harmony. Our mind is often beyond our control. It races from one idea to the next like a wild horse in the wind. Delusive mental activity is the source of all of our suffering. Although we may know this, we still find it very hard to control our mind.

The self and its desires are not in harmony. There are good desires and bad desires. Good desires can improve the self, and even benefit others. However, if we poorly manage these desires, they may become burdens. Bad desires, such as coveting material things and being attached to physical desire, create even more suffering than when we mismanage our good desires. We may understand that desire produces karma and suffering, but that does not mean the mind will be able to control itself easily. Self-control is difficult precisely because what we know to be best for us is not always what we most want. If we do not even bother to control our desires, but instead give them free rein, then the self will suffer even more.

The self and its views are not in good harmony. This basically means that we have wrong views or false perceptions. When what we believe is not in accordance with the truth, we cause ourselves endless trouble because we will be prone to repeat the same mistakes over and over again.

The self is not in harmony with nature. Rain, flood, droughts, storms, waves, and all of the other forces of nature are beyond our control and often can cause us to suffer.

The Buddha taught the truth of suffering not to make us despair but to help us clearly recognize the realities of life. When we understand the extent of our suffering and the impossibility of avoiding it, we should feel inspired to overcome it.

THE SECOND NOBLE TRUTH

The Second Noble Truth is the truth of the causes of suffering. The origin of the causes of all suffering is greed, anger, and ignorance, also known as the three poisons. Sentient beings chain themselves to the painful and delusive phenomenal world through their strong attachments to these three poisons.

THE THIRD NOBLE TRUTH

The Third Noble Truth is the truth of the cessation of suffering. "Cessation of suffering" is another term for nirvana, a state that cannot be described by language. It is beyond greed, anger, ignorance, and suffering, and it is beyond all duality and all distinctions between right and wrong, self and other, good and bad, and birth and death.

THE FOURTH NOBLE TRUTH

The Fourth Noble Truth is the truth of the path leading to the cessation of suffering. The way to the cessation of suffering is the path that shows us how to overcome the causes of suffering and leads to nirvana. The most basic way to overcome the causes of suffering is to follow the Noble Eightfold Path.

THE IMPORTANCE OF THE FOUR NOBLE TRUTHS

The Four Noble Truths were the first teachings of the Buddha, and they were among his last teachings. When he neared his death, the Buddha told his disciples that if any of them had any doubt about the validity of the Four Truths, they should speak up and have their questions answered before it was too late. The close attention that the Buddha paid to the Four Noble Truths throughout his forty-five years of teaching shows the importance he placed on them.

When the Buddha was teaching the Four Noble Truths, he explained it three times from three different angles in order to help us better understand his message. These three explanations are called the "Three Turnings of the Dharma Wheel of the Four Noble Truths."

The first time the Buddha taught the Four Noble Truths is called the "First Turning of Dharma Wheel" or "Turning the Dharma Wheel for Recognition." During this "turning," the Buddha explained the content and meaning of the Four Noble Truths to his disciples so that they may understand its importance. He said, "Thus is suffering, which is oppressive. Thus is the cause of suffering, which is accumulating. Thus is the cessation of suffering, which is attainable. This is the path, which can be cultivated."

The "Second Turning of the Dharma Wheel" is also called "Turning the Dharma Wheel for Encouragement." In this assembly, the Buddha taught the methods for cultivating the Four Noble Truths and encouraged his disciples to practice these methods in order to sever their afflictions and attain liberation. The Buddha said, "Thus is suffering; you should understand. Thus is the cause of suffering; you should end. Thus is the cessation of suffering; you should attain. Thus is the path; you should practice."

The "Third Turning of the Dharma Wheel" is also called "Turning the Dharma Wheel for Realization." Here, the Buddha showed his disciples that he had already realized the Four Noble Truths, and encouraged them to diligently practice so that they too could realize these truths. He said, "Thus is suffering; I have known. Thus is the cause of suffering; I have eradicated. Thus is the cessation of suffering; I have realized. Thus is the path; I have practiced."

The Buddha is sometimes called the "Great Doctor" because his teachings can cure us of our diseased attachment to delusion. The best way to end suffering is to understand the Four Noble Truths. If the Four Noble Truths are properly understood, then the rest of the Buddha's teachings will be much easier to understand. If the Buddha's teachings are understood and practiced, they can lead to liberation from all suffering and pain. The Buddha is the doctor and he has the medicine. All we must do is take that medicine. The Four Noble Truths constitute the Buddha's most basic cure for human suffering.

Chapter Five

KARMA

Karma is a Sanskrit word that means "action" or "deed." It is a universal Law of Cause and Effect concerned with intentional deeds. The Law of Karma tells us that all intentional deeds produce results that eventually will be felt by the doer of the deed. Good deeds produce good karmic effects and bad deeds produce bad karmic effects. Karma operates at more than just one level. Individuals have karma, groups of people and societies have karma, countries have karma, and the earth as a whole has karma.

When we say that a person "has" karma, we mean that person's life is conditioned by the Law of Karma in such a way that his present circumstances may be understood to be results of his past behavior(s). The same can be said of groups of people, countries, and the earth we inhabit.

The concept of karma is central to all schools of Buddhism and all interpretations of the Dharma. No one could possibly understand Buddhism without fully understanding the concept of karma. The Buddha divided karma into three types: karma generated by the body, karma generated by speech, and karma generated by the mind. All intentional acts of body, speech, and mind produce karmic retribution that will inevitably occur. Even a Buddha cannot change the Law of Karma.

For most people, karma works through cyclic repetition. A certain intentional act produces a certain karmic result. Then this result is reacted to, and this reaction leads to another karmic result, and so on and so forth. Our lives are built upon our own reactions to conditions we have created ourselves. By reacting to our own karma over and over again, we mire ourselves in delusion. The Buddha said that the cycle of birth and death is a delusion that we cling to because we are not able to see beyond it. He said that we do not understand how to escape it because we do not understand how the cycle works. More than anything else, it is karma that keeps sentient beings trapped in the cycle of birth and death. However, if the Law of Karma is truly understood, it leads sentient beings to liberation from this cycle.

For the purpose of this discussion, "bad" means that which harms sentient beings while "good" means that which helps them. Good karma leads to rebirth as a human being or a heavenly being. On the other hand, bad karma is any action that harms and causes suffering to self or others. Very bad acts produce karma that leads to rebirth in one of the three lower realms of existence (the realms of hell, hungry ghosts, and animals).

Karma is the power that forces us to be born even if we do not want to be born and forces us to die even if we do not want to die. When we speak of the cycle of birth and death, it is important to understand that what is being cycled and recycled is not "we" but our karma. Buddhist practice places great emphasis on doing good deeds because the good that we do today will form the foundation for our lives in the future. The right way to understand karma is not to think about what we are getting today but rather what we are doing today.

THE DIFFERENT KINDS OF KARMA

Generally speaking, karma is divided into three basic kinds: the karma of body, speech, and mind. Whenever we form an intention in our minds, we have planted a mental karmic seed. As soon as we act on that intention, we have added more seeds to that first seed.

Good Karma, Bad Karma, and Neutral Karma. Some acts produce good karma, some produce bad karma, and some produce neutral karma. Good karma is produced by acts that are intended to help other sentient beings. This includes protecting all animals, giving charity, speaking kind and encouraging words, and thinking compassionate thoughts. Bad karma is produced by acts that are intended to harm self or others. For example, killing, stealing, sexual misconduct, lying, speaking harsh words, anger, greed, and wrong views all create bad karma. Unintentional acts produce neutral karma, which are actions that have no good or bad consequence. These actions also include involuntary behaviors like sleeping, walking, breathing, and eating.

Guiding Karma and Detailed Karma. Guiding karma might also be called determined karma. Guiding karma is the karma that determines whether one is born as a human being, an animal, hungry ghost, and so on. Detailed karma is also known as personal karma, the karma that determines the differences in physical appearance, personality, health, lifespan, and external circumstances (such as which family and nation one will be born into).

Collective Karma and Individual Karma. Collective karma is karma that is shared by many different beings at once. For example, human beings are born on this earth because they have the same karmic causes, and therefore, share the same result. The nation and region in which we live is also part of our collective karma. If our region experiences a flood or an earthquake, it too is a karmic result we share with the people who live in our area.

Collective karma can be further divided into "karma that is shared by all" and "karma that is not shared by all." When an earthquake strikes an area, everyone in that area is affected in some way by the earthquake. This is called "collective karma that is shared by all." However, each individual in that area will be affected by the earthquake differently. Some may be injured, some will not. Some may lose their homes, while others experience no damage at all. This is called "collective karma that is not shared by all." The same distinction could be made for a car accident or any other event that affects more than one person. In the same car accident, one person may be killed whereas another walks away unharmed.

Individual karma is karma that is different from person to person. For example, people may have different reactions to and emotions about one situation. Individual karma is also divided into "shared karma within individual karmas" and "non-shared karma within individual karmas." In a family, each member has different individual karma. However, when there is a shared situation such as a death in the family, the rest of the family members all feel pain and grief. This is called "shared karma within individual karmas." When two strangers meet on the street, they may share the same situation, but do not share the same reaction to it. This is called "non-shared karma within individual karmas."

Definite Karma and Indefinite Karma. Definite karma is karma that will result at a determined time and place, and cannot be avoided by any means. Indefinite karma is karma that has an indefinite result. This is because the right conditions have not yet ripened, so the time, place, and means of karmic retribution have not been determined.

The Four Types of Karma. We can further divide karma into four types as another way to help us understand its workings. The four types are: black-black karma, white-white karma, black-white karma, and neither-black-nor-white karma. Black karma refers to bad karma. Since black karma can only produce bad results, it is called "black-black karma." White karma refers to good karma. Since white karma can only produce good results, it is called "white-white karma." "Black-white karma" is a mixture of good and bad karma. "Neither-black-nor-white karma" might also be called "karma without outflow." This is karma that has severed all defilements and led to liberation. Awakened beings who have transcended the duality of "good" and "bad" or "black" and "white" no longer produce good or bad karma.

THE ORDER IN WHICH KARMA ARRIVES

The relationship between cause, effect, and the Law of Karma is very complex and difficult to understand, and yet it has a definite order. It is very important to have some understanding of this basic order because without it, people often lapse into the belief that there is not such thing as cause and effect, or karma. Without understanding the order in which karma arrives, it is too easy to see good people suffering hard deaths and bad people enjoying easy lives, and from this, concluding that there is no justice in the world and that there can be no such thing as karma. The truth is, karma arrives in a more or less definite order. We can distinguish three basic levels to this order: the first level is the karma generated in this life arriving in this life; the second level is the karma generated in this life arriving in the next life; and the third level is the karma generated in this life arriving in some life beyond the next life.

These different levels can be compared to different kinds of plants. Some seeds can be planted in the spring and their fruit can be harvested in the fall, while others may take a year or more to bear fruit. Some trees may not bear fruit for many years.

Karma arrives in different lifetimes for two basic reasons: the cause of the karma is either quick or slow to generate and the conditions of the karma are either weak or strong. Karmic causes that are quick or slow to generate are like plant seeds that may generate in a year, two years, or five years. Weak or strong conditions are like the conditions that may or may not surround one of those seeds. If a quick generating seed is given good light and sufficient water, it will grow very quickly, whereas a slow generating seed that is kept in the dark may not grow for many years.

Therefore, good people may suffer badly in this lifetime. This is because the bad karmic seeds that they planted in previous lives have ripened. Although they might have performed good deeds in this lifetime, the karmic causes of those good deeds are weak and the right conditions are not yet ripe, so they must wait for a future lifetime before they can reap good karmic retribution. Applying the same principle, people who do bad things may have good lives. The seeds they are planting today will bring them misery in the future, but before that day comes, they are receiving the results of good deeds done in past lives.

There are two basic principles that underlie all karma: all karmic causes and effects do not disappear, and bad karma and good karma cannot cancel each other out. The only way to avoid bad karmic retribution is to not plant bad karmic seeds. As long as we plant the seeds, they will remain in our consciousness and eventually bear the karmic fruits when the right conditions arise. Even though bad karma and good karma cannot cancel each other out, if we perform more good deeds we can lessen the effect from our bad karma and cause our good karma to ripen more quickly. This is like diluting salty water by adding fresh water so that the resulting water is less salty.

There are three other factors that determine the order or direction of our karma: the weight (seriousness) of karma, the habitual tendency of karma, and the intentional direction of karma. The effect of the weighty karma, whether good or bad, arrives before less serious karma. Our habitual tendencies are grooves that determine the direction our life. The habitual tendencies we have in this life will be a powerful force in determining the nature and quality of future lives. The third factor, the intentional direction of karma, refers to karma that is decided by the direction of our thoughts and intentions. When we go for a walk and come to an intersection, we may not know whether to go north, south, east, or west. At this moment, we may suddenly remember that we have a friend who lives on the west side. This thought then affects which direction we go in. In our lives, we should keep in mind that a single thought may lead us to hell or bring us closer to the Buddha.

PRINCIPLES AND EXPRESSIONS OF KARMA

The Buddha said that all phenomena are impermanent. If all things are changing moment by moment, and if nothing is eternal, why does karma continue throughout many lifetimes? According to the Buddhist sutras, the Buddha answered this question by comparing karma to "seeds" and "persistent traits."

A seed may be stored for many years, but as soon as it

meets with the right conditions, it will begin to sprout, then grow, bloom, and bear fruit. Over time, its flowers will produce more seeds. And these seeds, after meeting with the right conditions, will grow again. Karma works in the same way, for all of our intentional acts produce seeds that are stored in our consciousness. When the conditions are right, those karmic seeds will sprout and grow.

Karma is also like a "persistent trait." Our karma is like the fragrance that persists in the bottle even after the perfume has been used up. The habits, tendencies, and karma of one life will persist into the next life in a similar way.

From the above, we can understand the following principles: once a karmic seed has been made, it cannot be destroyed; the karmic result is a direct reflection of the karmic cause; and we alone must bear the effects of our own karmic causes.

This is to say, all sentient beings are trapped in the ocean of the cycle of birth and death due to karma. Karma is like the string that holds prayer beads together. The string connects all the beads; likewise, karma connects our lives from the past to the present and into the future, continuously causing us to be reborn in the six realms of existence. Therefore, our physical bodies are born and die, but "life" does not end. When we break a teacup, the pieces of the cup cannot be put back together. However, the contents inside the cup do not diminish even when they flow onto the table and then to the ground. Karma is like the tea that does not disappear; rather, it continues to exist in another incarnation. In this cycle, each person must bear his or her own good and bad karmic results. Gods or heavenly beings cannot reward us, and the King of Hell or demons cannot mete out punishment.

Since karma is created by each person and not controlled by the gods, everyone is equal under the Law of Karma. In fact, karma should bring us hope. For example, doing good deeds is like depositing money in a savings account. If we do not keep on saving, there will come a day when our money is all used up. Therefore, we need to continue to accumulate good karma by performing good deeds. Conversely, if we commit many bad deeds, it is like being heavily in debt. So long as we can change and turn to the good, we will one day be able to pay back what we owe.

From the Law of Karmic Cause and Effect, we know that all sentient beings are reborn in the ocean of birth and death, and that they are also related to each other. This kind of understanding will give rise to the mind of great compassion. By applying the Law of Karma with great compassion, we will not only have a happy life in this lifetime but also be reborn into a higher realm in the next life.

Chapter Six

THE THREE DHARMA SEALS

Buddhists say that all ultimate truths must be defined by four basic characteristics: they must be universal, they must be inevitable, true from the beginning, and eternally true. For example, all people are born and all people must die. This is an ultimate truth because it is true not just for Chinese, Indians, Australians, or Americans, but for all people at all times. Birth and death are universal and inevitable; this was always true in the past and will always be true in the future.

The Three Dharma Seals possess all four of these ultimate qualities. The Three Dharma Seals are as follows: "All phenomena are impermanent," "All phenomena do not have a substantial existence," and "Nirvana is perfect tranquility." These concepts are basic to all traditions of Buddhism. The Three Dharma Seals are also the source by which to affirm the Dharma, and the standard by which to distinguish between the true Dharma and non-Dharma. We can prove them to ourselves through reasoning and observation.

Impermanence, lack of a substantial existence, and nirvana are called the "Dharma Seals" because all things are "stamped" with them. There is nothing that does not possess these three ultimate characteristics. Another reason that Buddhists call these three truths "Dharma Seals" is that they are similar to official seals that prove documents are real and not forged. If any so-called "truth" contradicts the Three Dharma Seals, then it cannot be an authentic teaching of Sakyamuni Buddha. Any "truth" that is not stamped with all three of the Three Dharma Seals cannot be true. Even if the Buddha himself were heard saying a "truth" that contradicts the Three Dharma Seals, that "truth" could not be true. In this same vein, any truth that is stamped with all of the Three Dharma Seals must be true, whether a Buddha said it or not. These principles are so fundamental to Buddhism that it can further be said the any truth that is stamped with the Three Dharma Seals is a Buddhist truth and can be taken to be part of the Dharma.

The meaning and significance of the Three Dharma Seals is close to that of dependent origination, which is most representative of the teachings of the Buddha. They are another way of looking at truths that are fundamental to reality. Therefore, if we can fully understand them, we will be able to grasp the fundamental philosophy of Buddhism.

THE FIRST DHARMA SEAL

The First Dharma Seal says that all phenomena are impermanent. This means that all phenomena change; nothing stays the same. All phenomena are constantly interacting with each other, constantly influencing each other, and constantly causing each other to change. The First Dharma Seal also says that "the three time periods" (past, present, and future) flow continuously. Each and every phenomenon is changing from one instant to the next. They arise and cease within each moment.

For example, sentient beings experience birth, sickness, aging, and death. The world's environment changes from season to season and from year to year. Stars are born, exist, and die. Thoughts also arise, abide, and extinguish. Everything is like this: from moment to moment the phenomenal world moves constantly among the four states of being born, abiding, decaying, and dying. Nothing is permanent. This is the First Dharma Seal.

According to Buddhist sutras, there are two basic kinds of impermanence: momentary impermanence and periodic impermanence.

Momentary Impermanence. In Buddhism, a *ksana* is the smallest unit of time. Within the context of how we measure time today, it is approximately one seventy-fifth of a second. The *Record of Investigations of Mysteries* states, "A *ksana* is a 'moment' of thought. A single snap of the fingers contains sixty moments."

Therefore, a *ksana* is indeed an extremely brief moment of time. In the world, the phenomena that change most quickly are the thoughts in our mind.

According to the *Commentary on Abhidharma*, "In one day, there are 6,400,099,980 *ksanas* worth of the five aggregates arising and extinguishing." The *Rain of Treasures Sutra* says, "This deluded mind is like running water; it rises and falls without ceasing. Like lightning, the moments come and go without ceasing."

The thoughts in our mind are constantly changing from one moment to the next. All material things, from the time they are new until they have become old, do not suddenly change. Rather, these changes are constantly occurring from one moment to the next. This is why we say it is momentary impermanence.

Periodic Impermanence. During long periods of time, all phenomena are constantly changing from moment to moment, and as a result, finally extinguish. This process is what we call periodic impermanence. In fact, periodic impermanence is just an accumulation of "momentary impermanences." The process of birth, aging, sickness, and death in sentient beings; the process of arising, abiding, changing, and extinguishing in all things; the process of formation, abiding, decay, and emptiness in the universe; all gradually change from moment to moment. These gradual changes accumulate to a certain point, and then suddenly there is a marked change.

Understanding the First Dharma Seal is important because once we recognize the brevity of life and the impermanence of all situations, we will feel motivated to delve even deeper into the truths of Buddhism. Impermanence should not frighten us but rather inspire us to appreciate our time on earth. We should understand that as difficult as life may be, we should always try to live a good life.

The *Great Nirvana Sutra* says, "All phenomena are impermanent. Loved ones who come together must one day separate."

Recognizing the impermanence of all things can inspire us to help all sentient beings realize the Buddha nature within.

THE SECOND DHARMA SEAL

Not only are all phenomena impermanent, but they are also devoid of a "substantial self." Having "no-self" nature means that all phenomena depend on other things for their existence. Nothing is independent and able to exist without other things. The word "phenomena" includes both formed and formless things, all events, all mental activities, all laws, and anything else you can think of.

To say that nothing has a self is to say that nothing has any attribute that endures over long periods of time. There is no "self" that always stays the same. If the "self" cannot possibly stay the same, then how can it really be a self?

This Second Dharma Seal goes right to the heart of human psychology. You may say that you do not believe that anything has a self, but chances are you will act and think as if you did believe it. Human thought patterns generally gravitate toward absolutes: things are the way they are, they have always been that way, and they will stay that way. Solid things seem permanent to us. Our sense of self seems immutable. "I am what I am," and "I" will stay that way.

The truth is that "we" are always changing, just as everything else is always changing. Not only do things not have a self, but neither do we. Most of the world's religions maintain the exact opposite. They claim that an absolute, eternal, and completely perfect "god" created human beings and their eternal souls.

Buddhism denies "self" in two basic ways. First, it states that sentient beings are without "self." Most people are very attached to their bodies, and this attachment leads them to believe that there is some absolute essence inside of them that is the "real" self. The Buddha said that the body is formed by the five aggregates and the accumulation of karma. It is a "temporary form" caused by a brief congregation of the physical and mental components of existence. As a house is made up of many parts that create a form, the body is also made of many components that create a substantial existence. Once those parts are separated, no real self will be found anywhere.

Second, Buddhism teaches that all phenomena are without self. Phenomena arise due to other phenomena. When the causes and conditions that produce and uphold them are removed, all phenomena themselves will cease to be. To say that phenomena have no self is another way of saying that they arise dependent on one another. It is important to understand these basic ideas because they are fundamental to all Buddhist practice.

THE THIRD DHARMA SEAL

Nirvana is the Third Noble Truth: the cessation of suffering. According to the *Commentary on the Flower Ornament Sutra*, "Nirvana means cessation." The *Great Nirvana Sutra* also says, "Cessation of all suffering is called nirvana." Since suffering is caused by delusion, nirvana is the cessation of delusion; since suffering is caused by the belief in duality, nirvana is the cessation of duality. Nirvana is also the cessation of the belief in a substantial self and the cessation of the birth and death of that "self." Because there is no more suffering, nirvana is the state of perfect tranquility.

When we say nirvana is the state of perfect tranquility, it refers to the state in which greed, anger, ignorance, arrogance, and doubt are eliminated. It is the state in which the body does not commit unwholesome deeds and the mind does not have unwholesome thoughts. It is the state of liberation.

Buddhists generally understand nirvana in four basic ways: nirvana of pure intrinsic nature, nirvana with remainder, nirvana without remainder, and nirvana without abiding. Nirvana of pure intrinsic nature is also called "originally pure nirvana." It is the "original" nature of everything and the Buddha mind that lies at the heart of everything.

Nirvana with remainder describes the state of an enlightened person who still has a physical body. "With remainder" means that the body with past karma still remains. An enlightened person is liberated from all defilements of the mind and creates no new karma, but his physical body still retains the karmic retribution from the past.

Nirvana without remainder is the state in which the defilements of the mind have been eliminated, and there is no future karmic retribution. In this state, an enlightened "person" is no longer subject to the cycle of birth and death.

Finally, nirvana without abiding is the fourth classification of nirvana. Because the bodhisattvas have great wisdom and have severed all defilements, they do not dwell in our world. And also because they have great compassion for all sentient beings, they choose not to enter the state of perfect tranquility. Therefore, this state of not dwelling in our world and not entering perfect tranquility is known as nirvana without abiding.

Buddhist sutras also speak of a state called "complete, perfect, and unsurpassed enlightenment." This state is basically the same as nirvana but is usually defined as "the Dharma-body of the Buddha." The term "Dharma-body" has many meanings. For now, it is sufficient to understand Dharma-body as "the body of the enlightenment of the Buddha." The *Lion's Roar of Queen Shrimala Sutra* says, "The Dharma-body is the great nirvana-body of the Buddha."

The great nirvana is the "Dharma realm of all Buddhas." It is the deepest *samadhi* of all Buddhas. It is a "state of blissful purity" that only a Buddha has fully attained. The *Lotus Sutra* says, "Only the Buddha has attained the great *bodhi*. This state of complete and perfect wisdom is called great nirvana."

Nirvana is the Buddha nature that all sentient beings possess. When the Buddha first became enlightened under the *bodhi* tree he exclaimed, "Wonderful! Wonderful! All sentient beings everywhere possess the wisdom and virtues of the Buddhas! But because of their delusions and attachments, they cannot attain [this wisdom and merit]. If they free themselves from delusions, perfect wisdom will manifest naturally."

Sakyamuni Buddha taught the Three Dharma Seals to help us eliminate our defilements or impurities. Contemplation of the Three Dharma Seals helps us overcome our attachments to delusion because the Three Dharma Seals cut off delusion at its three primary points. They teach us to understand that all phenomena are impermanent and devoid of a substantial existence. At the same time they teach us that contemplating these truths should not lead us to despair because all sentient beings possess Buddha nature. In the *Lotus Sutra*, the Buddha says, "I speak of the Three Dharma Seals to benefit all sentient beings in the world."

HOW TO UNDERSTAND THE THREE DHARMA SEALS

People sometimes think that Buddhism is a pessimistic religion because it talks so much about "emptiness," "impermanence," and "suffering." The Buddha spoke of these basic truths not because he was pessimistic but because he wanted people to fully understand the true nature of delusion. The Buddha knew that once delusion is understood, it loses its powerful hold over us. Once we see delusion for what it is, we will want it to "settle" or to "cease" so that higher levels of awareness can be born. The Three Dharma Seals should never make us despair. They should only help us transcend despair permanently.

Only Impermanence Can Give Us Hope. Most people instinctively react negatively to the First Dharma Seal. They think that impermanence means only that the "good will turn bad." While this may be true in some cases, it is just as true that the "bad can turn good." Impermanence is a great source of hope, for it teaches us that as hard as our present circumstances may be, they can change. If we are busy planting good seeds, then the changes that will inevitably come will be changes for the better, not the worse.

Properly understood, the concept of impermanence can be a great aid in difficult situations. If we are poor, impermanence can teach us that our circumstances will not last forever. If we meet with a setback in our work, it can teach us not to despair. If we meet with hardship or tragedy, impermanence can teach us that one day, things will change again for the better. Impermanence tells us that nothing stays the same; it teaches us that things can change for the better if we truly work to better our circumstances.

Another very good effect that comes from contemplating impermanence is that we learn to treasure what we have. Impermanence teaches us to be grateful for every moment of life and to use our time as productively as we can. It reminds us that if we do not make progress in Buddhism now, we may have to wait many lifetimes before we encounter the Dharma again. Impermanence inspires us to progress, study, and learn, for now is the time to act because the present is all the time that we really have.

No-Self Teaches Us How to Cooperate. The basic reason Buddhists emphasize the lack of a self in anything is to help each one of us get past the almost narcissistic devotion we normally feel toward our body and the deluded belief that the body "proves" that there is some absolute "self." Attachment to love of self is the root source of all delusion. It produces anger and greed as it keeps us bound firmly to ignorance. Contemplation of the Second Dharma Seal will teach us how to break the binds of self-love. A human body is produced by conditions, and it is made up of physical and mental components. When conditions bring those components together, a body is formed. When those same conditions disperse, the body will cease to be. There is no substantial existence or absolute self present anywhere in the body.

From the time we are born to the time we die, all of us change all of the time. There is nothing eternal or permanent about us. Knowing this can be a great help if we find ourselves trapped in adverse circumstances. Contemplation of no-self can disarm deep-seated and painful feelings that arise from the erroneous belief that we posses an "eternal self" that really can be threatened, or insulted, or defamed. The *Great Technique of Stopping*

[*Delusion*] *and Seeing* [*Truth*] says, "When there is no wisdom, we will perceive the self as real. When we contemplate with wisdom, the self will be recognized as unreal."

In understanding the concept of no-self, it is important not to fall into the mistaken belief that you as a person are not here or that you do not exist. Most Buddhist beliefs and ideas should be understood on at least two different levels. One level is called the "mundane level" while the other is called the "supramundane level." The truth of no-self lies primarily on the supramundane level. This level helps us to understand the mundane world in which we all must live. The mundane world is more or less what everybody believes. We all must learn to function capably at this level because our languages and societies are constructed around this notion of the "self." At the same time, if we know that ultimately this mundane level is full of delusive thinking, our ability to function in it will be greatly enhanced. The truth of no-self should be used when it can help us understand life, but it should not become a prism that is used to distort life or an excuse to avoid life.

Properly understood, the truth of no-self helps us enter fully into life because it provides a firm basis for cooperation with other sentient beings. The Second Dharma Seal teaches us how to get along with others because it shows us very clearly that just as we are sustained by many conditions so others are too. In the same way that we need others, they need us too. Buddhism places great emphasis on all sentient beings. The Buddha spent forty-five years teaching the Dharma. None of us should believe that the truth of no-self is a reason to abandon other beings for a life of complete seclusion. On the contrary, the Second Dharma Seal should be understood as a primary reason to involve ourselves in our communities and to live fully among the other sentient beings. When we see "others" as "ourselves" and ourselves as just one part of a much larger life, then, and only then, will we have fully understood the Second Dharma Seal.

Nirvana Is the Ultimate Refuge. Most people believe that nirvana is attained only after death. Actually, nirvana is beyond birth and death. It is the state where the attachment to self and phenomena is extinguished, the state where all afflictions and defilements are eliminated, and the state of liberation from the cycle of birth and death. For example, a criminal who is shackled loses his freedom. Likewise, sentient beings are bound by the chains of greed, hatred, and ignorance. If they practice the Dharma and put an end to these defilements, then they will all be liberated and, thus, attain nirvana.

Some people say that life is like an ocean in which there is perpetual motion with waves coming one after another. The continuous movement of the ocean exemplifies the impermanence of all phenomena. If we can look at the waves through the eyes of the Buddhist sages, we can then understand that although the waves are turbulent, the nature of water is always calm. Likewise, life is an endless cycle of birth and death, but our intrinsic nature always abides in a state of perfect peace. Thus, if we want to attain the liberation and tranquility of nirvana, we have to realize it in the impermanence and non-substantiality of all phenomena.

To be in nirvana is to be beyond all time and space, all duality, all delusion, and all fear. Nirvana is the ultimate refuge of all conscious life. Nirvana is always the same and always present.

To understand the Third Dharma Seal is to understand that nirvana is the pure Buddha mind, the truth that lies at the center of all of the Buddha's teachings. One does not need to wait for death to experience nirvana because nirvana is always present in everything.

Chapter Seven

EMPTINESS

Buddhism has been called the "Gate to Emptiness" since ancient times because emptiness is one of its most important doctrines. Emptiness is also one of the characteristics that distinguishes Buddhism from other religions.

When the Buddha attained enlightenment under the *bodhi* tree, he awakened to the universal truth of dependent origination. Dependent origination means that everything in the world arises from causes and conditions, and that nothing has a substantial existence. The characteristic of all phenomena having no substantial existence is called "emptiness."

The word "emptiness" is an English translation of the Sanskrit word *sunyata* or the Chinese word *kong*. In Buddhist terminology, emptiness is closest to describing the ultimate reality of all phenomena. However, because many people do not understand what Buddhists mean by emptiness, they misinterpret it and believe that Buddhism is a religion of pessimism and seclusion. In fact, emptiness embraces the boundless universe, and true emptiness is able to give rise to all existence. Emptiness is not negation; it is emptying the mind of the notions of relativity, duality, and all phenomenal distinctions, even of our attachment to emptiness. We will then attain the state of ease, the state of liberation, and the state without the duality between emptiness and existence.

THE TRUE MEANING OF EMPTINESS

The *Treatise on the Middle Way* says, "Because there is emptiness, all dharmas exist. Without emptiness, all dharmas could not be." Without emptiness, the phenomenal world could not exist. Let's use a piece of cotton cloth as an example. From the perspective of dependent origination, the piece of cloth is "empty." Why? The cloth is only a "temporary appearance" because it is conditioned by other things. The cloth is made from cotton yarn, and the yarn is made from cotton fiber. Cotton fiber comes from cottonseeds, and the seeds need soil, air, sunlight, water, and nutrients before they can grow into plants that produce cotton. Therefore, the cotton cloth is the result of the combination of cottonseeds and conditions in the universe. Looking at all things from this point of view, we can see that the cloth's essential nature is empty. This is why we say that emptiness gives rise to all phenomena.

Emptiness is an ultimate truth. It can connect the Three Dharma Seals together. For example, nothing in the world is permanent and everything is always changing. This is the First Dharma Seal of "all phenomena are impermanent," which means that because of impermanence, the nature of suffering is empty. Nothing in the world has an "independent nature" and everything relies on one another for their existence. This is the Second Dharma Seal of "all phenomena have no-self," which means that because of dependent origination, the nature of phenomena is empty. Nothing in the world has true concreteness and perfect tranquility, and everything is like a dream, illusion, bubble, and shadow. This is the Third Dharma Seal of "nirvana is tranquility," which the Buddha taught to help sentient beings achieve liberation. It demonstrates how wondrous existence manifests true emptiness.

Emptiness is an essential part of a wonderful and profound philosophy, but it is impossible to convey the meaning of emptiness in a single sentence. The *Explanation of the Treatise on the Awakening of Faith in Mahayana* speaks of the "ten meanings of emptiness." Even though no one will ever be able to perfectly describe emptiness in any language, these "ten meanings of emptiness" can point our mind in the right direction and bring us closer to understanding what Buddhists mean by emptiness. Let us look, then, at these ten explanations:

1. Emptiness obstructs nothing. Like space, it pervades everything but does not obstruct anything.

2. Emptiness embraces all places. Like space, it spreads everywhere and there is nowhere it is not.

3. Emptiness is equal in everything. It has no preference for one thing over another.

4. Emptiness is immense. Like space, it is vast, without limits and boundaries.

5. Emptiness is formless. Like space, it has no shape or form.

6. Emptiness is pure. It is always pure, without defilements.

7. Emptiness is motionless. Like space, it is always still, away from arising and extinguishing, formation and decay.

8. Emptiness is absolute negation. It completely negates all things that have limits.

9. Emptiness is empty. It completely negates the substantial existence of all things and destroys all attachments to it.

10. Emptiness is ungraspable. Like space, it cannot be caught and held.

DIFFERENT KINDS OF EMPTINESS

In Buddhist literature, many kinds of emptiness are discussed. However, emptiness can be classified into three basic kinds. First, there is emptiness of the self, which is also known as emptiness of sentient beings. Since the life of all sentient beings is interconnected and dependent on causes and conditions, no single part of it can be said to have substantial existence in and of itself. Second, there is the emptiness of all phenomena. All phenomena are the result of causes and conditions, and have no substantial existence, so it is also called "phenomena without self." Third, there is supreme emptiness, which is beyond the duality of existence and emptiness, and does not abide in either existence or emptiness. Supreme emptiness is also called the emptiness of suchness, and means "nirvana of perfect tranquility."

The *Treatise on the Perfection of Great Wisdom* says, "In the state of nirvana, there is no form of nirvana. The emptiness of nirvana is supreme emptiness.... It leads all phenomena to the 'emptiness of suchness,' and is called supreme emptiness."

HOW TO RECOGNIZE EMPTINESS

In most people's minds, existence and emptiness are opposite concepts, that existence is not empty and emptiness cannot have existence. However, in Buddhism, emptiness and existence are two sides of the same coin, namely that all phenomena are empty because no substantial existence can be attained, and all phenomena have existence because the manifestation of existence is not empty.

How are we to recognize emptiness? From the manifestation of existence, we can recognize emptiness. The following are seven angles from which to approach this truth:

Continuous Succession. Nothing in the world is permanent or unchanging. All phenomena only exist in continuous succession. At any moment, they are arising and extinguishing. The cells of our bodies are an example of this. They are always changing, dying, and being replaced by new cells. Everything in the world is like this. The ancient saying, "In the Yangzi River, the waves from the back push the waves in front forward; a new generation of people replaces the old" illustrates that all things exist in continuous succession and are impermanent without substantial existence. From the continuous succession and impermanence of phenomena, we can understand the truth of existence is emptiness.

Cycles in the Phenomenal World. Everything in the universe is subject to the Law of Cause and Effect; therefore, it is empty. Let us take a fruit seed as an example. If the seed is properly planted in the earth and receives sufficient sunlight, air, water, and other nutrients, it will grow into a plant, produce flowers, and then bear fruit. The seed is the cause, and the fruit is the effect. When the seed from this fruit is exposed to the necessary external conditions and once again grows into a plant bearing fruit, the fruit that was originally the effect becomes the cause of a new life. Causes lead to effects, and effects become causes. From these incessant cycles, we can understand emptiness.

Components Coming Together. All phenomena are the coming together of causes and conditions. For example, our body is composed of flesh, blood, sinew, and many other components. If we separate all the constituent parts, the human body would no longer exist. Therefore, through the concept of components coming together, we can understand emptiness.

Relative Existence. All things exist in relation to other things. For example, in a three-story building, when a person walks from the first floor to the second floor, the second floor is "upstairs," the first floor is "downstairs." When that person walks from the third floor to the second floor, the second floor now becomes "downstairs." Therefore, what is "upstairs" and "downstairs," "above" and "below" is not absolute. All things exist only in relation one to another. This is another way to understand emptiness.

Temporary Appearances. Since there is no fixed standard, things are empty. Let's take light as an example. Whether it is a candle, a gas lamp, or an electric lamp, there is no fixed standard for brightness. If we light a candle in the dark, we may consider the light from the candle is bright. Yet, compared to the light from a lamp, the candlelight is no longer so bright. So, as we can see, there is no fixed standard for "brightness." From the lack of fixed standards, we can understand emptiness.

Temporary Names. The myriad phenomena in the universe have different names or labels. Take a piece of cloth as an example. If we wear it over our upper bodies, we call it a shirt. If we wear it over our legs, we call it a skirt or a pair of pants. If we wear it on our feet, we call it socks, and if we wear it on our heads, we call it a hat. It is the same piece of cloth, but it is called by different names. These names are also temporary, so they are empty.

Different Perspectives. Perceptions and perspectives are not fixed, and therefore, are empty. On a snowy evening, a poet sitting by the window is inspired by the beauty of the scene. He exclaims, "If it snows a few more feet, it will be even more beautiful!" At the same time, a homeless person huddled and shivering under the awning laments, "If it snows a few more feet, how will I be able to make it through the night?" Although they face the same scene, due to their difference in their perspectives, they have different perceptions. Therefore, through the concept of different perspectives, we can understand is emptiness.

THE WONDROUS FUNCTION OF EMPTINESS

The *Sutra of Magnificent Mysteries* says, "Without emptiness, there is no form. Without form, there is no emptiness. The two are like the moon and the moonlight; from beginning to end, they are always together¡K" Only when the nature of all phenomena is empty can phenomena manifest; only when all phenomena have a temporary appearance can they reveal that their intrinsic nature is empty. Existence is not existent outside of emptiness; emptiness is not empty outside of existence. Emptiness and existence always work hand in hand.

Some people say that in Buddhism, emptiness is like an X-ray. With an X-ray, we can see into the hidden depths of the body. Through the truth of emptiness, we can see into the reality of all phenomena.

Emptiness is like the digit zero. The nature of zero is nothingness, but if we place a zero after a one, we get ten. If we add another zero, we get one hundred, and another gives us one thousand. From this, we can see that although zero may seem useless, it can become very useful. Emptiness is also like that. Although some may say that emptiness is nothingness, in fact, the emptiness in the universe can embrace everything.

We can experience emptiness in our everyday lives. For example, a "baby girl" gradually grows up and is called a "little girl." When she gets into her teens, she is known as a "young woman." After she reaches her twenties or thirties, she is called a "Miss," and if she marries, she is known as "Mrs. So-and-so."

Having children, she becomes a "mother." When her children grow up and get married, she will gain more roles such as "mother-in-law" and even "grandmother." From the shift and changes in these "titles," we can understand the truth of emptiness.

Beautiful and ugly, old and young, big and small are all relative terms and have no absolute standards. They are but temporary names. The *Diamond Sutra* says, "Suchness has no form." It also says, "Phenomena have no absolute standard." Only emptiness is suchness; it is the "unchanging Dharma." Only when we realize emptiness, will we truly understand the world. When we understand emptiness, we will transcend all duality, and thereby, have a world that is more open and profound.

CONCLUSION

Most people think that because Buddhism talks about emptiness, it encourages us to negate everything. In fact, the Buddhist concept of emptiness is not negating at all. To the contrary, emptiness is the basis of the arising of all phenomena. It is not void; it is constructive. Without space, we would not be able to build a house. If a bag were not empty, it could not contain anything. Without emptiness in the universe, human beings would not be able to survive. Hence, there must be emptiness before there can be existence. All phenomena in the universe are built upon the basis of emptiness because emptiness is the essential principle for the existence and operation of phenomena. If there were no emptiness, all phenomena could not come into existence from conditions, and there would be no arising and extinguishing.

Emptiness does not mean pessimism and nihilism. It carries with it creative and constructive meanings. Once we fully recognize emptiness, we will be able to abandon the attachments that we cling to, and investigate all phenomena from new angles. When we can fully understand emptiness, we will be able to eliminate our biases and re-examine our lives again. If we have experienced and realized emptiness, we will be at harmony with all phenomena in the universe.

Chapter Eight

MIND

The mind is the essence of our spirit. It is without arising and extinguishing. It is the Dharma-body of all Buddhas and the wisdom-life of all sentient beings. The nature of the mind embraces all merits, virtues, and wisdom, and is away from delusions and attachments. All sentient beings have a mind, but its nature cannot be revealed because it is concealed by our ignorance and delusion. If one can know the mind, one will grasp its profound functions. How are we to know our own mind then?

WHERE IS THE MIND?

The mind neither comes nor goes. It has neither direction nor location. It is not inside, nor is it outside. It is not in between. It leaves no trace anywhere. In the *Surangama Sutra*, there is a section in which Ananda and the Buddha have a dialogue about the location of mind. Ananda, the Buddha's attendant, puts forth seven different locations, and the Buddha refutes each one in turn. Ananda asks the Buddha, "Does mind reside in the body? Does it reside outside the body? Is it hidden in the sensory faculty? Is the mind located inside the body when we close our eyes? Is it located where causes and conditions come together and where existence arises? Is it located between the sensory faculties and the six sense objects (six dusts)? Is it not abiding?" In his answers, the Buddha shows Ananda again and again that mind cannot be located nor pinned to any one of these places. If this is so, then where is the mind located?

The mind leaves no trace anywhere, but when we need it, we can see that it is everywhere. There is a saying, "It is neither inside, outside, nor in between. With the manifestation of all states and circumstances, the mind is completely present." The mind penetrates all things and permeates the ten directions; it is in all places and is present at all times. Where then, do we go to find the mind?

The mind cannot be found in form and cannot be sought through any traces. There is nowhere without mind, and there is also no time it does not exist. Then, where is the mind?

During the Chinese Tang Dynasty, Chan Master Huairang visited Chan Master Songshan An one day and asked him, "What is the meaning of the patriarch coming to the West?"

An turned it around and asked, "Why don't you ask yourself?"

Huairang then asked, "What is the meaning of self?"

An replied, "Pure contemplation and secret function."

Huairang inquired, "What is the secret function?"

Chan Master An instructed him by opening and closing the eyes. At that moment, Huairang had a great awakening.

That which performs the actions of opening and closing is our physical eyes; that which gives the commands is our true mind. Every minute, this mind is not separated from us, but most of the time it is ignored by us. Therefore, this mind is also called the "secret function," which means that it is not obvious, and in fact, exists without our awareness. A Buddhist verse says, "If you want to know the 'original self,' you must examine and investigate it directly. In everyday use, it is not even separated by a line."

THE NATURE OF THE MIND

Mind is formless. It has no size, shape, sound, nor smell. It cannot be touched nor held. Although the mind cannot be grasped like other objects, when it responds to phenomena and conditions, it will appear. The ancients used to say, "If you want to understand what the mind is like, it is neither long nor short, neither blue nor white. If you want to see the mind, open your eyes and it is there, close your eyes and it is there. This side is mind and that side is mind."

Mind is our true nature. It is our Buddha nature. We do not see it because it is like a dusty mirror covered by attachments and delusions. The mind with defilements is called the "deluded mind." The *Sutra of the Eight Realizations of the Great Beings* says, "Mind is the source of evil. Form is the gathering place of sin." When the sutras speak about the mind in this way, they are referring to the deluded mind that is attached to defilements. This is what we call the mind of sentient beings. On the other hand, when the mind faces a state or situation that it does not cling to, it is pure and carefree. This is the true mind, also known as the Buddha mind.

Imperial Master Zhongfeng (1263-1323) said, "There are several kinds of mind. What is called the physical mind resides in our bodies and is part of what we inherited from our parents. What is called the conditioned mind distinguishes between good and bad, positive and negative conditions that appear at the moment. What is called the spiritual mind transcends all worldly distinctions without confusion and without changing. This mind is luminous, pre-eminent, and unique. It is not increased among the sages and is not decreased among ordinary people. In the ocean of birth and death, it is like a pearl that illuminates the sea. On the shore of nirvana, it is like a moon that hangs in the sky."

The *Sutra Describing the Five Sufferings* says, "The mind evokes hell. The mind evokes hungry ghosts. The mind evokes heavenly beings. All actions and appearances are created by the mind. Those who can control their minds are the most powerful. I have struggled with my mind for countless eons. Today, I can attain Buddhahood and escape from the Three Realms all because of the mind."

Buddhist sutras use many metaphors and similes to help us understand the nature of the mind. In the following sections, I will discuss ten of these metaphors in some detail.

1. The mind is so hard to control that it is like an ape. The ancients used the saying, "the mind is like an ape and a thought is like a horse" to describe our mind. The ordinary mind is like an energetic and restless ape whose nature is active. It jumps

around and runs wild in the jungle without a moment of rest.

2. The mind moves as fast as a flash of lightning and sparks from flint. Nothing moves faster than the mind. From moment to moment, it races through the dharma realms without any obstructions. For example, you may think about traveling to Europe, and in an instant, scenes of Europe will appear in your mind faster than a bolt of lightning.

3. The mind is like a wild deer chasing sight and sound. When the deer is thirsty, it goes to a stream. When it is hungry, it searches for grass. Our mind is like the wild deer, unable to resist the temptations of the five desires and six dusts. It spends most of its time chasing after sights and sounds of the mundane world in order to fulfill ordinary appetites.

4. The mind is like a thief who steals our good merit. The sutras often compare the body to a walled city, the five sense organs to city gates, and our mind to a thief. It carries away our virtues and merits just as a thief might carry away the hard-earned savings of the people in the town. The Chinese scholar, Wang Yangming (d. 1173) said, "It is easy to capture the bandit in the mountains; it is difficult to catch the thief in the mind." If we can tame our minds, we will become the master of the mind and also increas our merits.

5. The mind is like an enemy that causes our body to suffer. Our mind is the enemy who is always causing trouble and making us suffer. The sutras say, "The nature of bad karma is empty. It is created by the mind. If and when the mind disappears, the karma is gone." Some people say, "Our bad karmas are so deep and heavy." From this, it may sound as though karma is permanent and unchangeable. But from the perspective of nature, we know that all phenomena are empty and without substantial existence. The nature of karma is the same. Therefore, bad karma is not unalterable. If we can repent our wrongdoings with a sincere mind, we can lessen our bad karma. Our mind always possesses Buddha nature, which is pure and at ease. But due to our various deluded thoughts, we suffer. If

we can eliminate these deluded and destructive thoughts, we can become friends with this enemy.

6. The mind is like a servant of affliction. The mind is like a servant who is ordered about by worldly temptations, is attached to external circumstances, and creates various afflictions. The sutras say that our mind has three poisons, five hindrances, ten "knots," eighty-eight "driving forces," and eighty-four thousand afflictions. These hindrances and afflictions can cover up our wisdom, restrain our mind, and cause them to lose their clarity and freedom.

7. The mind is like a powerful king. The mind is the king of the body, so it has supreme power over all. It gives the commands to our eyes, ears, nose, tongue, and body. It also produces various sensory and perceptive functions.

8. The mind is like a spring that flows without end. The poet Li Bo (701-62) once said, "The waters of the Yellow River flow from heaven." Our mind is like the Yellow River in that it moves continuously. All over the world, people are now facing an energy shortage. With the ever-increasing demand for energy, people have endeavored to develop renewable energy sources like solar, wind, and hydropower. Sources of hydropower include dams, rivers, streams, or springs. Our minds are like these rivers and springs; the wisdom of the mind is like the running water. If we can efficiently apply the "running water" of the mind, we will be able to escape the fear of deficiency.

9. The mind is like a painter. The *Flower Ornament Sutra* says, "The mind is like a painter. It can paint anything." If the mind is pure and good, it will paint a face of beauty and tranquility. If it is evil, it will paint the face of a demon. According to an old Buddhist saying, "Appearances are born from the mind." When the mind becomes skillful enough of a painter, it can create a world of unlimited beauty and compassion.

10. The mind is like space without boundaries. The nature of the mind is like the vastness of space, which can embrace every-

thing. The *Flower Ornament Sutra* says, "If you want to know the state of the Buddha, you should purify the mind so it can be as vast as space." Space is boundless; it embraces all without selection. If we want to understand the state of the Buddhas, we should open our mind, extend as far as space, and eliminate any attachments. Then, we will be able to embrace all phenomena and help all the sentient beings in the universe.

Master Dadian (732-824) said, "The mind without any delusions is the true mind." When a thought arises in our mind, we should observe it. If the thought arises from the mind with purity, equality, compassion, and equanimity, this mind is the true mind. If it arises from the mind with delusion, attachment, jealousy, and arrogance, this mind is the deluded mind. All good thoughts come from the true mind; all bad thoughts come from the deluded mind. When we can attain the state in which every thought that arises is good, the true mind will be everywhere. But when every thought that arises is bad, the true mind cannot be revealed.

THE WONDROUS FUNCTION OF THE BUDDHA MIND

Everyone has a true mind. This mind is also called "the master," "the original self," "the Dharma-body," and "Buddha nature." No matter what we do, where we go, or what we think, this master is always with us. For example, when we are hungry, it reminds us to eat; when we are thirsty, it reminds us to drink; when the weather turns cold, it reminds us to put on more clothes. It cares for us as much as our mothers. This is what is meant by, "When seeing forms and hearing sounds, its great function appears before us; when wearing clothing and eating food, its great kindness and strength carries us."

Chan Master Deshan of Northern China, an expert in the *Diamond Sutra*, had written *The Blue Dragon Commentary on the Diamond Sutra*. He had heard about the Southern Chan School's method of "sudden enlightenment," and he heartily disagreed with it. Therefore, he decided to go to the South and debate this method, carrying *The Blue Dragon Commentary on the Diamond Sutra* with him. On the way, he passed by a small shop. In the shop was a little old lady. Seeing that Deshan wanted to buy some refreshments, she asked him, "What are you carrying on your shoulder?"

Deshan replied, "*The Blue Dragon Commentary on the Diamond Sutra*."

The old lady said, "Then, let me test you with a question on the *Diamond Sutra*. If you can answer it, the refreshments will be free."

Hearing this, Deshan confidently agreed.

The old lady continued, "The *Diamond Sutra* says, 'The past mind cannot be found. The present mind cannot be found. The future mind cannot be found.' May I ask you then: the mind that wants to eat refreshments, which mind is it?"

Deshan was stunned and did not know how to answer.

How could our true mind have differentiation of past, present, and future? Actually, the thought we have at this very moment is the wondrous function of the true mind. In conclusion, the mind is away from having and not having. Chan Master Hanshan captures the wondrousness of the mind in a poem. He writes:

> My mind is like the autumn moon,
> Clear and bright as a jade pool.
> Nothing compares to its beauty,
> How can I describe it?

Chapter Nine

NATURE

Since long ago, we have lived with someone who is closest to us. However, we do not know him by name. Who is he? He is our own Buddha nature. The saddest thing about us is that we do not know ourselves and do not recognize our own original face. Every day, we are able to call out our friends' names, but we do not know who we are.

We study Buddhism in order to know ourselves, to respect ourselves, and to affirm ourselves. The Buddhist sutras say that everyone possesses Buddha nature. It is not sought from outside; it is what everyone already has. When the Buddha attained enlightenment on the diamond throne under the *bodhi* tree, he said, "Wonderful! Wonderful! All sentient beings have the wisdom and merit of Tathagata. But because of their delusions and attachments, they cannot attain enlightenment."

When the Buddha held an assembly on Vulture Peak, he held a *mani* jewel in his hand and showed it to the four heavenly kings, saying, "Look at this *mani* jewel. What color is it?"

The four heavenly kings each answered differently: blue, yellow, red and white.

The Buddha took back the *mani* jewel. Then he opened his hand again and asked, "What color is this *mani* jewel in my hand?" The four heavenly kings did not understand and replied in unison,

"Buddha, there is no *mani* jewel in your hand!"

The Buddha said, "When I showed you an ordinary jewel, you could all distinguish its color. But when the true *mani* jewel was before you, you could not see it."

The wisdom and merit of the Tathagata and the true *mani* jewel are both like our own Buddha nature–we live with it every day but do not recognize it even when it is right in front of our eyes.

UNCHANGING NATURE

Nature, *prakrti* in Sanskrit, is the opposite of "appearance" and "cultivation." It means "unchanging." Nature refers to the original quality and the essence of all phenomena (intrinsic nature). Regarding phenomena with form, it refers to the "self-body" of matter or the innate quality of sentient beings. Nature is the quality that external forces cannot change and the essence that is present throughout the universe. It is the root of all phenomena. Nature is also known as Buddha nature, Dharma-body, the pure body of intrinsic nature, the nature of Tathagata, the nature of enlightenment, the original nature of the Buddha, and the awakening nature of sentient beings.

All phenomena in the universe have no substantial existence. Just as the universe has formation, abiding, destruction, and emptiness; people have birth, aging, sickness, and death; and the mind has arising, abiding, changing, and extinguishing. Only the original nature of phenomena and our own original face are never-changing.

Sentient beings have been transmigrating endlessly in the ten dharma realms, which are the realms of the Buddha, bodhisattva, *pratyeka-buddha*, the *sravaka*, the celestial beings, human beings, *asura*, animal, hungry ghost, and hell. Even when their forms of existence have changed, the nature of the mind does not change. This is like gold, which can be made into rings, bracelets, or earrings. It may take on many different forms, but the nature of gold has not been altered. Therefore, when sentient beings transmigrate in the five realms of existence, their original nature is the same.

When Master Huineng (638-713) was near death, all of his disciples who heard this news wept. Only Master Shenhui (668-760) remained calm and composed. So Master Huineng said, "Why are you crying? I am very clear on where I am going. If I did not know myself, how could I tell you beforehand? Only Shenhui has transcended the duality of good and bad, and reached the state without the arising of joy and sadness. All of you must remember: Dharma nature does not arise nor extinguish, come nor go."

Therefore, the patriarch said, "The mind turns following myriad circumstances, and the point of turning actually can be tranquil. If you can recognize the nature in this flow, you will be without joy, without sorrow."

DIFFERENT NAMES FOR BUDDHA NATURE

In the Buddhist sutras, many different words are used to denote Buddha nature. Master Jizang (549-623), in his *Commentary on the Mysteries of the Mahayana*, said, "The sutras speak of 'bright nature,' 'Dharma nature,' 'suchness (*tathata*),' 'reality,' and so on. All of these are different terms for Buddha nature." He also said, "Buddha nature has many names including 'Dharma nature,' 'nirvana,' '*prajna*,' 'one vehicle,' '*surangama samadhi*,' and 'lion roar *samadhi*.' It is said that the great sage follows conditions and applies skillful means. That is why there are so many names throughout the various sutras."

The following is a short list of names for Buddha nature in the sutras:

The *Sutra of Bodhisattva Precepts* calls Buddha nature the "mind ground" or the "ground of the mind." This "ground" can give rise to infinite goodness.

The *Sutra on the Perfection of Great Wisdom* calls Buddha nature "*bodhi*," which means "awakened" or "enlightened." It is because the essence of Buddha nature is awakening.

The *Flower Ornament Sutra* calls Buddha nature "*Dharmadhatu*," which means "Dharma realm." It is because Buddha nature unifies and embraces everything in the universe.

The *Diamond Sutra* calls Buddha nature "Tathagata," which is usually translated as "Thus-Come." It is because Buddha nature comes from nowhere.

The *Sutra on the Perfection of Great Wisdom* calls Buddha nature "nirvana." It is because nirvana is where all sages will return.

The *Sutra of Golden Light* calls Buddha nature "Tathagata" because Buddha nature is truly eternal and unchanging.

The *Vimalakirti Sutra* calls Buddha nature "*Dharmakaya*," which means "Dharma-body." It is because Buddha nature is what the delight-body and the transformation-body rely on.

The *Awakening of Faith in the Mahayana* calls Buddha nature "*Bhuta tathata*," which means "true essence." This is because Buddha nature does not arise and does not extinguish.

The *Great Nirvana Sutra* calls Buddha nature "the Buddha essence." It is because Buddha nature is the essence of the three bodies of the Buddha.

The *Sutra of Complete Enlightenment* calls Buddha nature the "universal embracing and upholding." It is because all merits and virtues flow from Buddha nature.

The *Lion's Roar of Queen Shrimala Sutra* calls Buddha nature the "storehouse of the Tathagata." This is because Buddha nature conceals, covers, and embraces all things.

The *Sutra of Supreme Meaning* calls Buddha nature "complete enlightenment." It is because Buddha nature can break through the darkness and illuminate all things.

We can say that it is "one Dharma, a thousand names" for responding to all circumstances.

The Chinese philosopher Mencius said, "The mouth turns to taste, the eye to form, the ear to sound, the nose to smell, the four limbs to peace and quiet. These are their natures." This is to say, the eyes can see, the ears can hear, the nose can smell, the tongue can taste, the body can move, and the consciousness can perceive. These are all functions of the true mind. With regard to sitting or sleeping, speaking or staying silent, moving or remaining still, carrying water or cutting firewood, receiving guests or sending someone off, all of them are from the heart of Buddha nature. Therefore, the patriarch said, "In the womb, it was the body. In the world, it was a human being. In the eyes, it sees. In the ears, it hears. In the nose, it smells. In the mouth, it speaks. In the hands, it grasps. In the feet, it moves. It appears throughout the dharma realms; it is contained in a speck of dust. Those who know this call it Buddha nature. Those who do not know this call it 'spirit' and 'soul.'"

THE EQUALITY OF BUDDHA NATURE

The Buddha said, "All beings who have the mind will eventually attain complete enlightenment (*anuttara-samyak-sam-bodhi*). Due to this reason, I always say, "All sentient beings have Buddha nature.'"

Master Huineng went from Guangdong Xinhui to Hubei Huangmei to ask Master Hongren (602-75) to become his teacher. When Master Huineng first met Master Hongren, the first thing Hongren asked him was, "Where do you come from?"

"I come from Lingnan," Huineng replied.

"Lingnan is a place of barbarians. Barbarians do not have Buddha nature," Hongren said.

Huineng then said, "People come from the north and the south. Does Buddha nature have a north and south?"

Although people are distinguished as southerners and northerners, wealthy and poor, Buddha nature does not have a south, north, wealthy, or poor. Towards all people, Buddha nature is equal. To all sentient beings, Buddha nature is like the rain that enriches the grass and the trees, sentient and non-sentient alike, without exception. So all sentient beings have Buddha nature, and Buddha nature is equal to all.

The *Dharma Method of Stopping* [*Delusion*] *and Seeing* [*Truth*] in Mahayana says, "If the essence of the mind is equal, there is no cultivation and no non-cultivation, achievement and non-achievement, or awakening and non-awakening. In order to clarify how bright the Buddha is, [the word] 'enlightenment' is used. Again, if the essence of the mind is equal, there is no differ-ence among sentient beings, Buddhas, and mind. Therefore, the verses in the sutra say, 'Mind, Buddha, and sentient beings have no difference.' Since the mind creates dharma realms due to dependent origination and Dharma nature is not destroyed, this results in the truths of eternal equality and eternal differentiation. Because of eternal equality, mind, Buddhas, and sentient beings have no difference. Because of eternal differentiation, when transmigrating in the five realms of existence, [nature] is called 'sentient being'; when returning to the origin, it is called 'Buddha.'"

Master Daoxin (580-651), the Fourth Patriarch of the Chan School, lived on Mt. Shuangfeng. On the mountain dwelled an old woodcutter who wished to become a monk under the Chan Master. Master Daoxin told him, "You are already too old. If you want to become a monk, you can wait until your next life."

The old man then left the master and walked to a stream where he saw a young woman washing clothes. The old man asked her, "Miss, may I stay the night?"

The young woman answered, "I have to ask my parents."

"I just need your permission, and it'll be all right," the old man said.

Just like that, the young virgin became pregnant. Because her parents felt that she had ruined their reputation, they kicked her out of the house. The young woman survived by begging. Eventually, she gave birth to a son.

Some years later on Huangmei Road, Master Daoxin encountered the little boy. This child requested to become a monk.

The Chan Master said, "You are too young. How can you become a monk?"

"Chan Master!" the child said, "In the past, you said I was too old. Now you accuse me of being too young. When are you willing to let me become a monk under you?"

The Chan Master suddenly had a realization. He immediately asked, "What is your name? Where do you live?"

"I am called 'the boy with no name.' My home is on Shili Alley."

"Everyone has a name," the master said. "How come you do not?"

The boy answered, "I take 'Buddha nature' as my name, so

I do not have a name." This boy without a name later would later be known as Master Hongren, the Fifth Patriarch of the Chan School.

In Buddhism, cause and effect of the three time periods and transmigration in the five realms of existence are truths of eternal differentiation. Because there is differentiation in our mundane world, there is a saying, "Too old, not wanted. Too young, not appropriate." However, when the "boy with no name" took Buddha nature as his name, he demonstrated that he understood the eternal and unchanging characteristics of nature. This is the truth of eternal equality.

In the *Record of Wanling*, Master Huangbo (d. 850) says, "The patriarch directly pointed out that the original mind of all sentient beings is the nature of the Buddhas, which does not need to be cultivated, does not have any levels, and is neither dark nor bright. The mind is the Buddha. From the Buddhas down to the beings with lower sentience, all possess Buddha nature and have the same essence of the mind. Therefore, Bodhidharma came from the West and transmitted only one Dharma. He pointed out that all sentient beings are essentially Buddhas and do not need to cultivate. Today, aside from recognizing the mind and seeing one's intrinsic nature, you must not seek."

In the *Lotus Sutra*, whenever Sadaparibhuta Bodhisattva was bullied, hurt, insulted, or scolded by others, he not only did not get mad, but he would respectfully say, "I dare not be disrespectful toward you, for I treat you all as Buddhas." From his example, we should understand that the equality of Buddha nature means that respecting others is the same as respecting oneself.

IGNORANCE AND ENLIGHTENMENT
AND BUDDHA NATURE

The *Awakening of Faith in the Mahayana* says, "The one Dharma is the one mind. This one mind embraces all mundane and supramundane dharmas. It is the Dharma method of the great oneness of one Dharma realm. It is only because of delusions that there are distinctions. Away from delusion, all that is left is such-ness." What this means is that as long as all sentient beings can stay away from and eliminate all delusions, they are Buddhas with pure intrinsic nature.

What is ignorance? It is when illusions become real and when we pursue our delusions. What is enlightenment? It is awakening to delusion and returning to the Truth. However, those who are ignorant cause their own ignorance, and those who are enlightened achieve their own awakening.

There was once a student monk who went to the place of Imperial Master Nanyang Huizhong (d.775) to study with him. He asked for instruction, saying, "The mind is the nature that is not increased in the Buddhas and not decreased in ordinary people. The patriarchs changed the term 'mind' to 'nature.' Please Chan Master, what is the difference between 'mind' and 'nature'?"

Imperial Master Huizhong said, "When ignorant, there are distinctions. When enlightened, there are no distinctions."

The student monk then asked, "Buddha nature is perma-nent. The mind is impermanent. Why do you say that there is no difference?"

Huizhong said, "You are only depending on the words and not depending on the meaning. For example, when it is cold, water turns into ice. When it is warm, ice melts into water. When you are ignorant, your nature freezes into mind. When you are enlight-ened, your mind melts into nature. Mind and nature are the one and the same. Due to ignorance and enlightenment, there is a differ-ence."

In the *Diamond Sutra*, the Buddha says, "*Prajna-paramita* (the perfection of wisdom) is not *prajna-paramita*. This is called the perfection of *prajna*-wisdom." It means, "What is Dharma is not Dharma. What is not Dharma is Dharma." These statements may sound like contradictions, but actually, whether it is Dharma or not Dharma depends upon ignorance and enlightenment.

One day, Chan Master Danxia Tianran of the Tang Dynasty stayed overnight at a Buddhist temple. It was winter. There was a heavy snowstorm and the weather was very cold. Danxia took a wooden statue of the Buddha and threw it into the fire. When the disciplinary monk saw this, he loudly reprimanded, "You should die for that! How dare you take the Buddha statue and burn it to stay warm?"

Danxia said, "I am not burning it to stay warm. I am burning it to obtain relics."

The disciplinary monk said, "Nonsense! How could a wooden statue have relics?"

"Since it is wood and has no relics, why don't you bring me more to burn?"

In the mind of Chan Master Danxia who had already realized the Law of Dependent Origination and the emptiness of nature, the Dharma-body of the Buddha pervades everywhere in the universe. The Buddha that the disciplinary monk recognized was only the wooden Buddha statue. Due to one thought of ignorance, what was once the pure Dharma becomes impure mundane dharma. Therefore, we say that Dharma is not Dharma.

Another Chan story illustrates this point. One day, Chan Master Panshan Baoji (720-814) of Youzhou Province was walking past a marketplace. Suddenly, he heard an exchange that caused him to awaken.

A patron said to a butcher, "Sir! Cut me a piece of good meat!"

The butcher laid down his knife. Hands on his hips, he said, "Dear fellow, tell me, which piece is not good?"

All phenomena arise from dependent origination. They are all equal, without distinctions and duality. Due to one thought of enlightenment, mundane dharmas become supramundane Dharma. This means that the ignorant mind is turned by the world, but the awakened mind transcends the world. The difference between ignorance and enlightenment is only based on one thought and whether it is transcendent or not. This is the cultivation of the mind, not oral debate. From the mundane dharma of selling meat, the Chan Master realized the truth that Dharma nature is equal and without duality. Therefore, we say that what is not Dharma is Dharma.

While a young person was meditating, an old Chan master happened to walk by. The young man did not rise to greet him, so the Chan master said, "You saw me coming. Why did you ignore me? So impolite!"

The young monk, imitating the Chan master's tone of voice, said, "Sitting to greet you is the same as standing to greet you."

When the old Chan master heard this, he immediately stepped forward and slapped the young man on each side of the face. After the young man was smacked, he held his face in his hands and protested, "Why did you hit me?"

The old Chan master, as if nothing had happened, said, "When I hit you, it is not hitting you."

Another story illustrates how much emphasis Chan masters place on understanding Buddha nature. When Master Heze Shenhui first met the Sixth Patriarch Huineng, Huineng asked, "You come from far away. Have you brought the intrinsic nature and the Chan mind? Can you see your own Dharma nature?"

Shenhui replied, "Master, 'I' have coming and going, but 'intrinsic nature' has no coming and going. The original Dharma nature permeates through all the dharma realms. How can we say we see it or do not see it?"

Master Huineng said, "What a quick-witted response!" and then hit him with the walking stick.

Shenhui asked in return, "When the master sits in meditation, do you see or not see?"

Huineng answered, "When I hit you, does it hurt or not hurt?"

Shenhui said, "I feel the hurt, but it also does not hurt."

Huineng said, "When I meditate, I see and do not see."

Shenhui asked, "Why is it seeing and not seeing?"

Huineng answered, "I see because I always see my own mistakes. I don't see because I don't see the right and wrong, the good and bad in others. So, it is seeing and not seeing. To the extent that you do not feel pain, then you are like wood or stone, and do not have feeling. If you feel pain, then you are like the average person who may have a resentful and angry mind. Therefore, seeing and not seeing are the two sides of attachment. Pain and no pain are the phenomena of arising and extinguishing. You are not even clear about your intrinsic nature, how can you say it is 'without coming and without going'?"

When one who has not yet attained enlightenment persists in imitating the way an awakened one speaks, this is just like the Six Patriarch's saying, "Shenhui's seeing and not seeing are the two sides of attachment. Pain and no pain are the phenomena of arising and extinguishing." But Buddha nature transcends all. To sever the two sides, to not distinguish between the good or the bad, is to truly see nature. From this, we can see the difference between ignorance and enlightenment.

Why are sentient beings ignorant then? It is because delusions cover our Buddha nature. Buddha nature is like the pure blue sky, without any pollution. Buddha nature is also like a clear mirror that has been covered by the dust of delusions and attachments, and so it has lost its own true nature. When this happens, we fall into the ocean of birth and death, and we suffer.

The meaning of this is perfectly captured in *Yongjia's Song of Enlightenment*:

> Do you not see?
> Leaving secular learning, acting with non-action, a care-
>   free person on the Way,
> Does not eliminate delusion, does not seek the Truth.
> The real nature of ignorance is Buddha nature,
> The transformed and empty body is the Dharma-body.
> Awakened to the Dharma-body, there is not a single thing,
> The origin of intrinsic nature is the true Buddha.

SEE ONE'S NATURE, BECOME A BUDDHA

The *Platform Sutra of the Sixth Patriarch* says, "Your original nature is like space. When not a single thing can be seen, this is called Right View. When not a single thing can be known, this is called true knowledge. Not having blue or yellow, long or short, but seeing that the origin is pure and clean, and the essence of enlightenment is complete and bright, is called 'seeing one's nature, becoming a Buddha.' It is also called the 'Tathagata's knowing and seeing.'" It also says, "When seeing all dharmas, if the mind is not deluded and attached, this is no-thought. When applied, it spreads everywhere but is not attached anywhere. Purifying the original mind, making the six consciousnesses go out the six gates, being without defilements and distractions in the six dusts, coming and going freely, and going everywhere without obstruction is "*prajna-samadhi*, freeness, and liberation." This is called the practice of no-thought."

What we mean is that Chan practitioners should take no-thought as their aim. Under all dharmas, they should not take nor give up, should not defile nor attach. They should follow their conditions naturally, and be free and liberated. This is the way to "see one's nature and become a Buddha."

Chan Master Huangbo Xiyun said, "If practitioners of the Way want to attain Buddhahood, they do not need to learn all Dharmas. They only need to learn to not seek and not attach. Not seeking is the mind without arising. Not attaching is the mind without extinguishing. Not arising and not extinguishing is the Buddha. Therefore, we must understand that all dharmas are created from the mind.... Today, learn no-mind, eliminate all conditions, do not give rise to delusions and distinctions, be without others and self, be without greed or anger, be without hatred or love, be without winning or losing, eliminate as many delusions as possible. The original nature is pure. This is the way of cultivating *bodhi*, Dharma, and Buddha. If you do not understand this and do not know the original mind, even if you widely study and diligently cultivate and even if you eat rough food and wear coarse clothing, you are on the wrong path."

When you can attain the state without seeking and attachments and the state in which all delusions are eliminated, you will see your own nature and become a Buddha.

Chapter Ten

NIRVANA

For thousands of years, many profound doctrines and teachings in Buddhism have been misunderstood. For example, "nirvana" is the state that all Buddhist practitioners want to attain, but many people mistakenly take nirvana to mean death. Actually, nirvana is not death. It is a transcendent state that is completely different from death. Nirvana is an eternal life, and a perfect and complete world.

In most Buddhist monasteries, statues of the Buddhas are usually depicted in three positions: standing, sitting, or lying down. The sitting position represents *samadhi* (meditative concentration), which is a state of stillness and self-benefit. The standing position represents the spirit of educating and liberating sentient beings, which is a state of action and benefiting others. The recumbent position is also called the "nirvana position," which represents the state of absolute perfection and auspiciousness. It is the unity of stillness and action. The state of perfection means liberation from birth and death, transcendence of all space and time, elimination of duality, and oneness of self and others. Therefore, nirvana is not death. It is the most valuable life, the most real life. It is the highest state of self-realization in Buddhism.

THE MEANING OF NIRVANA

In Sanskrit, the word nirvana means "extinction," "liberation," "tranquility," and "non-arising." The *Great Nirvana Sutra* says, "The extinction of all defilements is nirvana." The *Commentary on Abhidharma* says the meaning of nirvana is, "the elimination of all afflictions, the extinguishing of the three fires (greed, anger, and ignorance), the extinction of the three aspects of all phenomena, and the leaving of all realms of existence." The *Connected Discourses of the Buddha* says nirvana is "desire of greed forever ended, anger forever ended, ignorance forever ended, and all afflictions forever ended." Thus, nirvana is the third truth of the Four Noble Truths. It is a world in which greed, anger, ignorance, wrong view, duality, and affliction are all extinguished. It is a kind of tranquility and purity that transcends others and self.

When the Buddha became enlightened on the diamond throne under the *bodhi* tree, he awakened to the Truth of the universe and attained perfect enlightenment. This kind of perfect enlightenment is nirvana. Therefore, nirvana is our pure original nature; it is the true "self." If we can attain nirvana, we will be able to eliminate the tension between self and others, and transcend the obstruction of space and time. We will not be bound by afflictions, suffering, duality, differentiation, and hardships, and we will not be trapped in the cycle of birth and death. If we can enter this enlightened state, we will transcend birth and death into liberation.

DIFFERENT NAMES FOR NIRVANA

There are many words in Buddhist sutras and commentaries that are used to describe nirvana. With a total of forty-three different names for nirvana, the *Abhidharma-skandha-pada* says that it is "non-action, non-abiding, non-doing, without boundaries, without outflow, without arising, without extinguishing, without beginning, without defilements..." The *Treatise on the Four Noble Truths* explains nirvana in sixty-six different ways, as "without destroying, without loss, without equal, without hindrance, without desire, without anything above it, without limit, without attachment..." These are all negating terms used to describe the meaning of nirvana.

The *Abhidharma-skandha-pada* also says that nirvana is "truth, the other shore, marvelous, tranquil, eternal, secure, supreme, the most wholesome, unique..." with a total of fifty ways. According to the *Treatise on the Four Noble Truths*, there are forty-six different descriptions: "liberation, transcendent, the one and only, complete, pure, supreme, truth, suchness..." These are affirming descriptions that give nirvana broader interpretations.

In addition to these descriptions, the *Great Nirvana Sutra* says that Buddha nature is nirvana. The *Flower Ornament Sutra* says that the intrinsic nature of all phenomena is nirvana. The *Sutra on the Perfection of Wisdom* says, "*Prajna* that is beyond common knowledge and knows everything" is nirvana. The *Surangama Sutra* says "the Truth in which activity and stillness are ceased" is nirvana. The *Vimalakirti Sutra* says that "the Dharma method of non-duality" is nirvana. The *Lion's Roar of Queen Srimala Sutra* tells us that nirvana is the "storehouse of the Tathagata" and "the pure mind." Nirvana is the intrinsic nature that does not have arising and extinguishing.

In China, the great translator Kumarajiva translated nirvana as *miedu*. *Mie* means to extinguish the hindrance of defilements, and *du* means to go across the ocean of birth and death to the other shore. Xuanzang, another great translator in China, translated nirvana as *yuanji*. *Yuan* means complete and perfect, and *ji* means tranquility. Even though nirvana has been called by so many different names, the truth of nirvana is simply to have all merits and virtues, and eliminate all deluded habitual tendencies and afflictions.

SPECIAL CHARACTERISTICS OF NIRVANA

With regard to the explanations and interpretations of nirvana, although there are many different names and descriptions in the sutras, the truth of nirvana never changes. It always refers to the pure intrinsic nature and the essence of reality. This nature and essence is "not increased in the sages and not decreased in the ordinary." The *Universal Complete Nirvana Sutra* says that nirvana has eight characteristics: eternal abiding, extinction and tranquility, without aging, without death, purity, ubiquity, non-action, and joy.

1. Eternal abiding. Nirvana permeates the three time periods of past, present, and future and always exists. It pervades all ten directions and always abides in the universe.
2. Extinction and tranquility. In the state of nirvana, birth and

death are extinguished. It is also the state of total tranquility.

3. Without aging. Because it does not move, change, increase, or decrease, it is said to be "without aging."

4. Without death. Since nirvana never arises and ceases, it said to be "without death."

5. Purity. Since all defilements have been purified, nirvana is the state abiding in purity.

6. Ubiquity. Because it permeates everything without difficulty, nirvana is ubiquitous.

7. Non-action. Nirvana is completely tranquil and without action. Therefore, it is called "non-action."

8. Joy. There is no more suffering from birth and death in the state of nirvana. Only eternal happiness remains. Therefore, nirvana is also called "joy."

In the Buddhist sutras, similes and metaphors are also used to describe the state of nirvana. I will discuss ten of these comparisons below.

1. Nirvana is like a lotus flower. A lotus flower cannot grow away from mud, but it is also not soiled by the mud. Nirvana is like the lotus flower. It is not defiled by any afflictions, but it cannot be attained away from the cycle of birth and death.

2. Nirvana is like water. Nirvana has the refreshing and cleansing qualities of water; it can extinguish the fire and suffering of afflictions. Just as water can quench thirst, nirvana can relieve all desires.

3. Nirvana is like an antidote for all poisons. Nirvana is like the medicine that can cure all afflictions. Therefore, nirvana is the refuge for all sentient beings who are suffering from the poisons of defilements and afflictions.

4. Nirvana is like the great ocean. The great ocean can embrace all remains without differentiating between like and dislike. Nirvana is also far away from the remnants of defilement and has no attachment to love and hatred. The ocean is vast and

does not differentiate between this shore and that shore. It can embrace a thousand rivers without ever becoming full. Likewise, nirvana is also vast and without boundaries. It can embrace all sentient beings without ever becoming full.

5. Nirvana is like food. Food can satisfy our hunger and sustain us. Similarly, nirvana can wipe out the hunger and weaknesses of our suffering, and calm the worries and anxieties of sentient beings.

6. Nirvana is like space. Nirvana is a state that is without birth and death, without coming and going, and without attachments. Likewise, space is without boundaries and limits. It abides nowhere and pervades everywhere. It does not depend on anything, but everything relies on it.

7. Nirvana is like a *mani* jewel. Nirvana is like a *mani* jewel; it can radiate a glow of virtue. It brings joy to all sentient beings.

8. Nirvana is like sandalwood. Sandalwood is a kind of precious wood. Nirvana is like sandalwood; it can give off the fragrance of the precepts, with which nothing can compare. Nirvana exceeds all other things in the world.

9. Nirvana is like the wind. The wonderful quality of nirvana can blow people towards *bodhi*. Like a gust of wind, it can carry a sailboat across the sea.

10. Nirvana is like a mountain peak. Nirvana is like a mountain peak that stands firm amidst the wind and storms, and stands so tall that the thieves of defilement cannot climb up to the top. On the peak, the seeds of suffering and ignorance cannot grow.

THE DIFFERENT KINDS OF NIRVANA

There are different levels of nirvana. The different schools of Buddhism categorize nirvana in more than one way. In the following section, I will take the classifications of nirvana from the Tiantai and the Mind-Only Schools as examples.

Three Kinds of Nirvana. The Tiantai School classifies and interprets nirvana from three aspects: its essence, appearance, and application.

1. Nirvana as the purity of nature. From the aspect of its essence, the nature of all phenomena is pure, and does not arise and cease. This is why we say that this kind of nirvana has the purity of nature.

2. Nirvana as complete purity. From the aspect of appearance, nirvana is the fruit of cultivation in which the nature of all phenomena is truly realized and all defilements are completely purified. This is why we say nirvana is the state of complete purity.

3. Nirvana as skillful means. From the aspect of application, nirvana is the skillful means by which the Buddha teaches all sentient beings. In order to liberate sentient beings, the Buddha manifested the transformation-body and taught all Dharmas corresponding to the different conditions of sentient beings. When the right conditions ceased, his transformation-body entered nirvana. Actually, birth is non-birth; death is also non-death. The phenomena of birth and death are presented through the skillful means of nirvana. Therefore, it is also called "transformation nirvana."

Four Kinds of Nirvana. The Mind-Only School categorizes nirvana into four kinds.

1. Nirvana as pure intrinsic nature. Although all phenomena are covered by defilements, Dharma nature is always pure and unchanging, without arising and extinguishing, has immeasurable merits and virtues, and is equally possessed by all sentient beings. It is different from all dharmas; it is also not different from all dharmas. Sentient beings need not seek the attainment of pure intrinsic nature from outside. Therefore, we say this is nirvana that is pure intrinsic nature.

2. Nirvana with remainder. Although those who have attained nirvana with remainder have cut off the defilements of the Three Realms and create no new karma, their physical body that resulted from past karmas still exists. However, it is no

longer influenced by hunger, cold, suffering, and joy. In the face of human reality, those who attain nirvana with remainder always maintain a state of tranquility.

3. Nirvana without remainder. Those who have attained nirvana without remainder have not only cut off all defilements, but the physical body no longer exists. All remnants of past karma are gone.

4. Nirvana without abiding. Those who have attained nirvana without abiding have cut off the hindrance of attachment to the Dharma, and have realized the Truth that there is no difference between *samsara* (cycle of birth and death) and nirvana. Therefore, they have no aversion to *samsara*, return to suchness, and are not attached to abiding in nirvana. They use their great compassion and wisdom to benefit all sentient beings throughout the three time periods and across ten directions.

From the classifications described above, we can see that one does not need to wait until death to achieve the state of nirvana. The life of the Buddha provides a good example of this. When the Buddha was thirty-five years of age, he achieved nirvana while sitting under the *bodhi* tree. However, his physical body that was the result of past karma still existed. This came to be known as nirvana with remainder. When he was eighty years old, he passed away under twin *sala* trees, achieving nirvana without remainder. During the forty-five years of traveling to various places to teach the Dharma and liberate sentient beings, he lived a life without delusion and without attachment. This is "nirvana without abiding."

In the *Lotus Sutra*, the Buddha says about himself, "I became a Buddha many eons ago. From that time on, I have stayed in the *saha* world to teach the Dharma and liberate others. I also traveled to countless worlds to guide and benefit sentient beings."

That the Buddha was born, renounced, defeated the *maras*, attained Buddhahood, taught the Dharma, and entered nirvana in the *saha* world is the application of "nirvana as skillful means."

This is also the state of "nirvana without abiding." So, if we are seeking to attain nirvana, we must find our intrinsic nature. This is "nirvana as pure intrinsic nature."

THE STATE OF NIRVANA

Every day, sentient beings suffer from their own ignorance and craving in the world of five desires and six dusts. On the contrary, what state do the Buddhas and bodhisattvas who have attained nirvana dwell in? According to the *Nirvana Sutra of the Northern Tradition*, nirvana has four states, also called the "four virtues of nirvana." They are: eternity, bliss, true self, and purity.

1. Eternity. In the state of nirvana, awakening is a state that never changes. It is eternal.

2. Bliss. In nirvana, there are four kinds of bliss: bliss without suffering, bliss with great tranquility, bliss with perfect wisdom, and bliss that cannot be destroyed. In our world, happiness is tempered by suffering, and is therefore conditional. On the other hand, the state of nirvana transcends all suffering and happiness. This is where one attains absolute, perfect bliss without suffering. The state of nirvana is also beyond language, words, and thought. There is bliss with great tranquility because nirvana transcends the confusion and chaos of different points of view. After the Buddhas and Tathagatas attain nirvana, they gain great wisdom. Away from all delusions, they can then truly understand the truth of all dharmas. After the Tathagatas attain nirvana, their Dharma-body is like *vajra* (diamond); it cannot be destroyed.

3. True Self. When one attains the state of nirvana, the self is completely free, without limits and attachments. This kind of self is the true self.

4. Purity. In nirvana, delusions and defilements are extinguished. This state is perfectly clear and pure.

Nirvana is without arising, without abiding, without self, without lacking. It is the ultimate state that ends the accumulation of all suffering. It is the world that eliminates craving, abandons clinging, and ceases desires and afflictions. To enter nirvana is to enter the blissful land of complete virtues.

HOW TO ATTAIN NIRVANA

Nirvana transcends all duality in the phenomenal world. It cannot be attained through worldly experience, knowledge, and learning. It can only be attained through one's own cultivation and self-realization. From the teachings of the sages who have already attained nirvana, we know that there are three ways to reach this state.

1. Rely on upholding precepts. The *Questions of King Milanda* says, "If those seeking the Way are settled in upholding precepts and diligently cultivate, they can attain nirvana no matter where they dwell. This is like people who have eyes. They can see the sky no matter where they stand. Therefore, nirvana relies on upholding precepts." To reach nirvana, we should take the precepts as our teacher and diligently cultivate.

2. Rely on the Three Dharma Seals. If we want to achieve Buddhahood, we have to follow the Buddha's teachings. We must contemplate on the Three Dharma Seals; "All phenomena are impermanent. All dharmas are without substantial existence. Nirvana is tranquility." We have to understand that the nature of all dharmas is empty. With regard to all phenomena, we do not give rise to any thoughts of attachment and fear in the mind. We must cut off and end all delusions, and be without attachment and clinging. By accomplishing this, we will reach the state of nirvana in which all dharmas abide in tranquility and attachments are eradicated.

3. Rely on the three studies, the four means of embracing, and the six perfections. To attain the state of nirvana, we need to settle our body and mind with the three studies, which are: pre-

cepts, meditative concentration, and wisdom. In our practice, we must also use the four means of embracing—charity, kind words, beneficial actions, and cooperation—to liberate other sentient beings. Lastly, even in our most trivial activities, we must diligently cultivate a life of the six perfections by giving charity, upholding precepts, practicing patience, diligence, meditative concentration, and *prajna*-wisdom. We should always practice mindfulness, which will turn our ignorance into enlightenment.

CONCLUSION

As one of the Three Dharma Seals, nirvana is the ultimate goal in Buddhism. After the Buddha attained enlightenment, he came to clearly see that all sentient beings created bad karma due to their ignorance, transmigrated in the Three Realms, and suffered in the cycle of birth and death. With great compassion, he sought to help sentient beings free themselves from delusion and the suffering of birth and death, eliminate all their bad karma, and finally achieve the ultimate state of tranquility. This is the reason the Buddha taught us the truth of "nirvana is tranquility."

In the *saha* world, the human lifespan fleetingly lasts through a few decades of winter and summer, and the human body usually grows no more than seven feet tall. We face a life with limitations, but if we can attain nirvana, we will be able to transcend the limitations of time and space. We will overcome the fear of birth and death and the fear of impermanence. Our "life" will then permeate through all space and time, and we can achieve the state of absolute and complete happiness. Therefore, everyone should live each day with the mind to "attain nirvana and find the true self." We do this by treasuring every second of every minute, and diligently cultivating our mind.

Chapter Eleven

TAKING REFUGE IN THE TRIPLE GEM

Taking refuge in the Triple Gem is the first formal step onto the Buddhist path. Taking refuge signifies that we believe in Buddhism and that we have become disciples of the Triple Gem– the Buddha, the Dharma, and the Sangha. When we take refuge in the Triple Gem, it determines the direction of our faith. Buddhist practitioners who do not take refuge are but people who respect or have an interest in Buddhism. They cannot be considered true Buddhist practitioners.

Gold, silver, diamonds, and pearls are all considered to be treasures in our mundane world. In the world of Buddhism, the Buddha, Dharma, and Sangha are the treasures of our Dharma-body and wisdom-life. By making a commitment to the Triple Gem, we take the first step in our journey to learn and practice Buddhism.

THE MEANING OF THE TRIPLE GEM

The Triple Gem is the collective term for the Buddha, Dharma, and Sangha.

Buddha is the Sanskrit word for "enlightened one." It refers to the enlightened being who has awakened to the Truth of the universe and has vowed to teach other sentient beings the Truth, liberating them with infinite compassion.

Dharma, also a Sanskrit word, has many meanings. The Dharma we are speaking about here means the teachings of a Buddha. Usually, it refers to all of the written teachings contained in the *Tripitaka*, the *Buddhist Canon*. If sentient beings rely on the Dharma to cultivate, they will realize the Truth and attain the ultimate liberation.

Sangha is a Sanskrit word meaning "community in harmony." It refers to the community of monastics (monks and nuns) who follow the Dharma and live together in harmony. This harmonious community has two special characteristics: "harmony in [pursuit of] the Truth" and "harmony of action." Harmony in the Truth means that all monastics realize the same Truth. Harmony of action means that the monastics' three activities of body, speech, and mind must comply with the six principles that are the basis of establishing the Sangha. They are:

1. Doctrinal harmony in views and thoughts. In terms of ideas, there is the establishing of a common point of view. This is the harmonization of thought.
2. Moral harmony through upholding the same precepts. In terms of rules and regulations, everyone is equal. This is the equality of the precepts.
3. Economic harmony through sharing. In terms of material resources, benefits are equally shared. This is equal allocation of material goods.
4. Spiritual harmony through joy. In terms of spirituality, the same determination for the Way is shared. This is the blossoming of the mind.
5. Verbal harmony without disputes. In terms of speech, there is harmony without conflicts. This is the kindness of words.
6. Physical harmony by living together. In terms of conduct, there is no violation of others. This is the happiness of getting along.

From the view of benefiting self, the sangha is the great crucible for cultivating oneself, disciplining temperaments, and tempering the mind to sagehood. From the view of benefiting others, the sangha has the power to transmit the right Dharma and to liberate sentient beings. We can see the importance of the sangha in each of these areas.

To put it simply, the Buddha is considered to be the liberator, the Dharma the Truth, and the sangha the teacher. These three components are all important causes for the liberation of sentient beings. Not one can be lacking. Let us use the example of the

Buddha as the good doctor, the Dharma as the medicine, and the sangha as the nurse. For the patient, only by having the three elements come together can his illness be cured. This is also true in life, for only by relying on the Buddha, the Dharma, and the Sangha can we achieve joy without suffering and reach the state of liberation.

The "Triple Gem" is a metaphor that reveals the supreme virtues of the Buddha, Dharma, and Sangha. These three "gems" transcend all worldly treasures. They can relieve our mental suffering and lead us to liberation from *samsara*. According to the *Treatise on the Ultimate Precious Nature*, "The Triple Gem has six meanings, and we should respect them." The following section explains why the Triple Gem is so precious:

1. The Triple Gem is rare. Just as people who are poor may not be able to obtain worldly jewels, people who do not accumulate enough good conditions will not come across the Triple Gem.
2. The Triple Gem is without defilements. In the same way that the composition of a pure gem is without impurities, the Triple Gem is without defilements.
3. The Triple Gem is powerful. Just as gems like crystal have the power to cleanse impurities, the Triple Gem has powers to purify the mind and eliminate the three poisons of greed, anger, and ignorance.
4. The Triple Gem is dignified. In the same way that a jewel can beautify our appearance, the Triple Gem can dignify the original nature of practitioners.
5. The Triple Gem is supreme. Just as jewels are considered to be the most valuable things in the world, the Triple Gem is the most supreme in the universe.
6. The Triple Gem is immutable. In the same way that the nature of gold cannot be changed by melting or shaping, the Triple Gem cannot be changed by the gain, decay, destruction, fame, praise, ridicule, suffering, and happiness of the mundane world.

THE MEANING OF TAKING REFUGE

Taking refuge means that we return to and rely on the Triple Gem, seek protection from the Triple Gem, and attain liberation from suffering through the Triple Gem. Children rely on their parents for protection and safety. Many seniors rely on a cane to walk more steadily. Sailors rely on compasses so they can safely return home. In the dark, people rely on lights so they can see what is in front of them. Likewise, if we have the Triple Gem in our lives, we will have something safe to rely on.

The Triple Gem is also like a compass that can guide us in the great ocean of life towards a safe harbor. If we take refuge in the Triple Gem and learn to appreciate its merits, we can rely on it to cross the sea of suffering and to return to our true home-our original nature. Therefore, taking refuge in the Triple Gem can help us find a safe haven to settle in during this lifetime, and allow us to have a home where we can return to in the future.

THE BENEFITS OF TAKING REFUGE

The Triple Gem is the candlelight in the dark night. It is the boat navigating through the tides in the ocean of suffering. It is the rain that falls to put out the fire of a blazing house. Taking refuge in the Triple Gem not only allows us to attain ultimate liberation, but also gain the benefits in this lifetime. According to the sutras, there are ten benefits of taking refuge. They are discussed below:

1. We will become disciples of the Buddha. When we take refuge in the Triple Gem, we accept the greatest sage in the universe, Sakyamuni Buddha, as our teacher, and we formally become disciples of the Buddha.
2. We will not be reborn in the three lower realms. According to the sutras, when we take refuge in the Buddha, we will not fall into the realm of hells. When we take refuge in the Dharma, we will not fall into the realm of animals. When we

take refuge in the Sangha, we will not fall into the realm of hungry ghosts. By taking refuge in the Triple Gem, we can escape from the lower realms and will be reborn in the realm of humans or the realm of celestial beings.

3. It will dignify our character. When we don beautiful clothing, our appearance becomes more elegant. After we take refuge in the Triple Gem, our faith deepens and our character becomes more dignified.

4. We will be protected by the Dharma guardians. The Buddha instructed the Dharma guardians and all good deities to protect the disciples of the Triple Gem during the Period of Declining Dharma.

5. We will gain the respect of others. After we take refuge in the Triple Gem, we will receive respect from other people and from celestial beings.

6. We will accomplish good deeds. By relying on the strength and support of the Triple Gem, we will lessen our bad karma and gain peace and joy. We will then be able to achieve many good deeds in our lives.

7. We will accumulate merits and virtues. According to the sutras, even all the merits and virtues from making offerings and building stupas cannot compare with the merits from taking refuge. From this, we can see that the benefits of taking refuge in the Triple Gem are vast and supreme.

8. We will meet good people. Taking refuge in the Triple Gem can help us eliminate our troubles. We will have the opportunity to meet good people and become friends with them. No matter where we go, we will find assistance and make good connections.

9. We will lay the foundation for taking precepts. Only after taking refuge in the Triple Gem are we qualified to take the Five Precepts and the Bodhisattva Precepts for laypeople.

10. We can achieve Buddhahood. All who take refuge in the Triple Gem, even if they do not cultivate in this lifetime, will be liberated when Maitreya Bodhisattva comes to this world because they have faith and good connections.

THE DIFFERENT KINDS OF TRIPLE GEM

In the sutras, there are different classifications for the Triple Gem. The most common classification further divides the Triple Gem into three levels: Initial Triple Gem, Abiding Triple Gem, and Intrinsic Triple Gem.

1. Initial Triple Gem. The Initial Gem of the Buddha refers to Sakyamuni Buddha, who achieved enlightenment sitting under the *bodhi* tree and manifested thirty-two marks of excellence and eighty noble qualities. The Initial Gem of the Dharma refers to the Four Noble Truths, the Twelve Links of Dependent Origination, and the Three Dharma Seals, which the Buddha taught at Deer Park after he attained enlightenment. The Initial Gem of the Sangha refers to the Buddha's first five disciples: Kaundinya, Mahanama, Bhadrika, Vaspa, and Asvajit.

2. Abiding Triple Gem. After the Buddha entered *parinirvana*, all the images of the Buddha, all written scriptures, and all monastics that have existed up to the present day is what the Abiding Triple Gem refers to.

3. Intrinsic Triple Gem. At the very moment the Buddha became enlightened under the *bodhi* tree, he said, "Wonderful! Wonderful! All sentient beings possess the wisdom and virtues of the Buddhas! But because of their delusions and attachments, they cannot attain Buddhahood." Within our intrinsic nature, we already possess the immeasurable merits and virtues of the Triple Gem. All people have Buddha nature; this is the Intrinsic Gem of the Buddha. All people have Dharma nature that is equal and without differentiation; this is the Intrinsic Gem of the Dharma. All people have the nature of the mind that is pure and joyful; this is the Intrinsic Gem of the Sangha.

The act of taking refuge in the Triple Gem is the external force through which we are guided to recognize the true self, affirm the true self, further rely on the true self, actualize the true self, and finally find the Intrinsic Triple Gem within ourselves.

Each one of us is like a treasury. By taking refuge, we are discovering the treasures of our mind. When the Buddha was about to enter *parinirvana*, he instructed his disciples to "Rely on self. Rely on Dharma. Rely on no others." This is the true significance of taking refuge in the Intrinsic Triple Gem.

THE PROCEDURE OF TAKING REFUGE
IN THE TRIPLE GEM

The intention to take refuge in the Triple Gem arises from an inspiration deep within the mind that seeks the Way. However, people still need to have a formal ceremony to strengthen and secure their resolve. The act of taking refuge lets our sincere mind connect with the mind of the Buddha. The Buddha can then flow into our body and mind with his great compassion. A moment of taking refuge transforms into a lifetime of believing.

If we have a container full of filthy water, we will be not able to pour in any more clean water. Similarly, if our mind is filled with doubt, arrogance, and deluded thoughts, we not be able to accept the pristine Triple Gem. For this reason, the *Sutra of the Great Name* says that all who take refuge must first sincerely repent. Then, with a reverent and pure mind, kneel down and join palms. Before the Buddha, they make the commitment and say:

I, disciple (your name), unto the end of my bodily form, take refuge in the Buddha, the incomparably honored one. I, unto the end of my bodily form, take refuge in the Dharma, honored for being free from defilements. I, unto the end of my bodily form, take refuge in the Sangha, most honored among sentient beings. (Repeat three times.)

I have taken refuge in the Buddha. I have taken refuge in the Dharma. I have taken refuge in the Sangha. (Repeat three times.)

Taking refuge in the Triple Gem is our first step onto the Way of Buddhahood. This is why we must take refuge under a monastic who is properly qualified. In the *Treatise on the Perfection of Great Wisdom,* it says,

> When we are ready to take refuge and are prepared to cultivate ourselves, we must go before a monastic. This precept master will teach us the Dharma of 'good and bad' for distinguishing between right and wrong, to have joy for the good and aversion for the bad, and to open our mind. Then we accept the refuge and say, "I, disciple (your name), unto the end of my bodily form, take refuge in the Buddha, the Dharma, and the Sangha." (Repeat three times.) "I, unto the end of my bodily form, have taken refuge in the Buddha, the Dharma, and the Sangha." (Repeat three times.)

These vows are spoken twice during the refuge ceremony. When we say them the first time, we formally accept refuge from the Triple Gem. When we say them the second time, it is at the conclusion of the ceremony.

The procedure for taking refuge in the Triple Gem is briefly described below:

1. Pay respect to the Buddhas with three prostrations.
2. Invite the Master to preside over the ceremony.
3. Sing the "Praise of the Incense Offering."
4. Call on "Sakyamuni Buddha" three times.
5. Chant the *Heart Sutra.*
6. Take the vows.
7. Repent.
8. Formally take refuge.
9. Discourse on the Dharma by the Refuge Master.
10. Transfer of merits.
11. Bow to the Refuge Master.
12. Bow to the other masters in attendance.

ANSWERS TO BASIC QUESTIONS
ABOUT TAKING REFUGE

1. Do I need to become a vegetarian after taking refuge?

Taking refuge in the Triple Gem does not require you to become a vegetarian. Taking refuge is the declaration of your commitment to follow the Triple Gem. It has nothing to do with vegetarianism. Those who do not take refuge can become vegetarians. Likewise, those who take refuge do not have to be vegetarians. Taking refuge is not the same as taking precepts, for taking precepts involves a greater commitment and certain restrictions. There is only one requirement when we take refuge: "I follow Buddhism, and my confidence in it will never change." So, taking refuge in the Triple Gem is not about becoming a vegetarian, is not the same as taking the precepts, and furthermore, is not the same as becoming a monastic.

2. After taking refuge, can we still pay respect to deities and to our ancestors?

Those who take refuge can still pay respect to deities and to their ancestors. This is because taking refuge and paying respect are different. Taking refuge is a lifetime belief; paying respect is a momentary courtesy. When we meet someone of a different religion, we should still show respect to them by shaking hands or bowing. With regard to our ancestors and deities, we should also show our respect to them. However, respecting is not the same as believing. After we take refuge, we should be careful of being superstitious and instead seek the Truth.

3. Is taking refuge in the Triple Gem temporary?

Taking refuge in the Triple Gem is not a momentary showing of respect; it is committing to a lifelong belief. According to the *Precepts of Yogacara*, a day without taking refuge is a day without following the precepts. To be a true Buddhist practitioner, one must take refuge in the Triple Gem each day. This very act demonstrates that we, ourselves, do not forget we are Buddhist practitioners. By doing this, we deepen our own belief and plant the seeds that can grow into *bodhi*.

4. Does taking refuge in the Triple Gem mean that we worship the Buddhist masters?

Taking refuge does not mean that we worship the masters; it is paying homage to the Buddha, learning the Dharma, and showing respect to the sangha. We often see Buddhists who call themselves disciples of the Triple Gem, yet they only take refuge in one. They may only pay homage to the Buddha, but they do not learn the Dharma or show respect to the sangha. Some only study the Dharma, but do not pay their respects to the Buddha or the sangha. Others respect the sangha, but do not pay homage to the Buddha or learn the Dharma. There are even those who only make offerings to the master they took refuge from, or those who treat the Buddha as a deity and god to whom they pray for wealth, blessings, and good fortune. These people are not true Buddhist practitioners. True Buddhist practitioners should not only show respect to all three gems, they should treat all monastics as their teachers and attend Dharma centers to study the sutras, learn the Dharma, and be close to Dharma friends. This is the true disciple of the Triple Gem.

Aside from these things, those who take refuge in the Triple Gem must have Right View and Right Thought, believe in the Law of Cause and Effect, and "commit no evil, do good deeds." Only in this way can we receive the benefits of the Dharma and of Buddhism.

Chapter Twelve

TAKING THE FIVE PRECEPTS

Taking refuge is the first step to becoming a Buddhist practitioner. By taking the precepts, we put our beliefs into practice. After Buddhist practitioners take refuge, they should take a further step by upholding the precepts because these precepts are the root of all good Dharmas and the basis for all moral conduct in our world. When we follow the precepts, it is like students following the rules of their school or citizens abiding by the law. The only difference is that rules and laws are external forces that regulate our behavior. They are, therefore, considered to be enforced discipline. However, the Buddhist precepts inspire the inner force of self-regulation. This is considered self-discipline. In our lives, if we do not obey traffic laws when we are driving, we are always in danger of getting into an accident. Likewise, if we do not uphold the precepts, we may make mistakes all the time and bring ourselves misfortune. This is why it is important for Buddhist practitioners to take the precepts.

THE FIVE PRECEPTS

The Five Precepts are: no killing, no stealing, no lying, no sexual misconduct, and no taking of intoxicants. It is asked in the *Connected Discourses of the Buddha*, what it is to fully uphold the laity precepts. The sutra says that laypeople "should stay away from killing, stealing, lying, engaging in sexual misconduct, and taking intoxicants. Furthermore, they should not wish to commit them. This is called 'fully upholding the laity precepts.' We can see that the Five Precepts are the precepts that laypeople should uphold."

Although the precepts in Buddhism are divided into monastic precepts and laity precepts, the root of all precepts is the Five Precepts. Hence, the Five Precepts are also called the fundamental precepts of Buddhism.

No Killing. Not killing is not violating or harming the lives of others. From the most serious form of killing, which is to kill human beings, to the less serious cases of killing ants or mice, they are all still considered acts of killing. However, Buddhism is a religion that emphasizes human rights, so the precept of not killing specifically means to not kill human beings. Killing a person is committing one of the *parajikas* (grave prohibitions) according to the Buddhist *Vinaya*, and does not permit repentance. If we kill cockroaches, ants, and the like, we commit one of the *duskrtas* (wrongdoings). Although it still carries bad karmic retribution, it is different from killing a human being.

In addition, wasting time and destroying material resources are also ways of "taking life." This is because life is the accumulation of time, so when we waste time, it is like taking a life. Similarly, when we casually destroy material resources, it is also taking away life. This is because material resources are for all sentient beings, and require the efforts of sentient beings to bring about the right conditions for them to come into being.

The main purpose of this precept of not killing is to encourage us to nurture our compassion. The *Great Nirvana Sutra* says, "Those who eat meat cut off the seed of great compassion. Whether they are walking, standing, sitting, or lying down, when other sentient beings smell the odor of meat on them, it causes fear and terror." Some Buddhists become vegetarians because they cannot bear to harm the lives of chicken, duck, pigs, lambs, cows, fish, and other animals. However, many also become vegetarians for the sake of cultivating the mind of compassion.

No Stealing. Not stealing is not taking the property and belongings of others. To put it simply, when we take things that do not belong to us without permission, it is stealing. When we take the property of others by force in broad daylight, this is a more serious violation of the precept of not stealing. According to the *Vinaya,* if one takes something worth more than five *masa*, this act of stealing is a violation of one of the fundamental precepts.

In our daily lives, if we take paper, envelopes, pens, or other supplies from our workplace, or if we borrow things and do not return them, this behavior is called "impure conduct." Although it does not break a fundamental precept, we still have to pay the karmic retribution and be held responsible for it. Of all the precepts, the hardest to uphold is the precept of not stealing, because we often borrow things for a short period of time and do not ask for permission, or we take others' belongings and keep them as our own.

No Lying. "Lying" is saying words that are untrue. This includes being double-tongued, saying harsh words, and using flattery. Lying can be further divided into three kinds: a great lie, a little lie, and a lie of convenience.

A "great lie" is committed when those who have not attained enlightenment say they have attained enlightenment, or those who do not have supernatural powers claim they have supernatural powers. In addition, when we gossip about the faults of sangha members, especially the faults of monastics, this is considered a violation of the fundamental precepts.

A "little lie" is committed when you see something but you say you have not, when you do not see something but you say you have seen it, when something is right but you say it is wrong, when you know something but you claim not to know, and vice versa.

A "lie of convenience" is more commonly known as a "white lie." An example is when a doctor, considerate of the patient's feelings, withholds information from the patient about the severity of an illness. This kind of lie that is told for the sake of others is a "lie of convenience."

No Sexual Misconduct. Sexual misconduct is sexual behavior that violates the law or the rights of others. For example, rape, prostitution, polygamy, pedophilia, sexual slavery, adultery, and other sexual acts that harm and negatively affect our society are all violations of the precept of no sexual misconduct. In cases of unrequited love, if we do not commit any acts that harm the object of our desire, we do not break this precept. But many times, our mind becomes unclear, and we are disturbed by our desires and anxieties. This causes us to lose peace of mind. Since the purpose of upholding the precepts is to purify our body and mind, this kind of behavior is contrary to the purpose.

Sexual misconduct is the fuse that ignites the chaos of society. For example, the problems of incest and child prostitution are a disgrace to all of civilization. If all people could uphold the precept of no sexual misconduct, these situations would not occur. If all couples resolved to uphold this precept, then families would be in harmony and society would be at peace.

No Taking of Intoxicants. Not taking intoxicants refers to not taking substances that stimulate the senses, causing us to lose self-control and violate the morals of society. For example, alcohol, marijuana, opium, amphetamines, cocaine, glue, painkillers, and the like are all substances that we should abstain from. However, when the Buddha established this precept, it only applied to drinking alcohol.

In the first four precepts, the essential nature of the behaviors we must abstain from is immoral. The essential nature of drinking alcohol is not itself immoral, but it can cause people to lose self-control and engage in killing, stealing, lying, and sexual misconduct.

According to the *Commentary on Abhidharma*, there was once a layperson who, after getting drunk, stole his neighbor's chicken and broke the precept against stealing. He then killed and cooked the chicken, violating the precept against killing. When his neighbor's wife asked about it, he lied and said that he did not see the chicken, breaking the precept against lying. At this time, he noticed the beauty of the neighbor's wife, so he raped her and violated the precept against sexual misconduct. From this story, we can see that when people drink too much, they may lose their sense of shame, remorse, and self-control. As a result, they may commit the four serious crimes of killing, stealing, lying, and sexual misconduct. Therefore, we should uphold this precept and abstain from using intoxicants.

THE MEANING OF THE FIVE PRECEPTS

Although the Five Precepts are different, their fundamental spirit is "to not violate." When we do not violate others but respect them, we will have freedom. For example, to not kill is to not violate the lives of others, to not steal is to not violate the property of others, to not engage in sexual misconduct is to not violate the bodies of others, and to not take intoxicants is to not harm our own rational mind and thereby not violate others.

Most people think that taking the precepts imposes more restrictions. Some people may wonder why they should take the precepts and create more restrictions for themselves. Actually, upholding the precepts brings freedom and violating the precepts leads to restrictions. If we look carefully at why people have been imprisoned and lose their freedom, we will see that they have violated the five precepts. For example, murder, assault, and disfiguration are all violations of the precept against taking life; corruption, invading, burglary, blackmail, robbery, and kidnapping are all violations of the precept against stealing; rape, prostitution, abduction, and polygamy are all violations of the precept against sexual misconduct; slander, breach of contract, perjury, and threatening are all violations of the precept against lying; and selling drugs, using drugs, trafficking drugs, and abusing alcohol are all violations of the precept against using intoxicants. People who violate the five precepts will most likely be imprisoned and lose their freedom. Therefore, taking the precepts is also abiding by the law. If we can uphold the Five Precepts and deeply understand them, we will have true freedom. For this reason, the true meaning of upholding the precepts is freedom, not restriction.

Some people think that when we take the precepts we will inevitably break them, but if we do not take the precepts we do not have to worry about breaking them. The truth is, after taking the precepts, even if we break a precept, we will repent because we have a remorseful heart. Through this act of repentance, will still have the opportunity to be liberated. When those who do not take the precepts break a precept, they do not know to repent. As a result, they fall into the three lower realms. It is better to take the precepts and repent if we violate them, rather than to not take the precepts and break them. Yet, not taking the precepts does not mean we do not violate them when we do bad things. When we do not take the precepts and we violate them, we still have to bear the karmic retribution without a way to escape from it.

THE BENEFITS OF UPHOLDING THE FIVE PRECEPTS

The Five Precepts are the foundation of all humanity. When we take and uphold the Five Precepts, we gain endless benefits. According to the *Abhisecana Sutra*, when we uphold the Five Precepts we will receive the protection of twenty-five Dharma guardians. The *Moon Lamp Samadhi Sutra* says that those who uphold the precepts with a pure mind will gain ten kinds of benefit:

1. They will have the fulfillment of all wisdom.
2. They will learn what the Buddha learned.
3. They will become wise, and will not slander others.
4. Their *bodhi* mind will not regress.
5. They will be settled in the state of cultivation.
6. They will be free from the cycle of birth and death.
7. They will be able to admire the tranquility of nirvana.
8. They will have an undefiled mind.
9. They will attain *samadhi*.
10. They will not be lacking in the Dharma wealth of merits and virtues.

Aside from this, if we do not take life but rather protect it, we will naturally have health and long life. If we do not steal and instead give charity, we will enjoy wealth and good standing. If we do not engage in sexual misconduct and instead respect the integrity of others, we will have a happy and harmonious family. If we do not lie but rather praise others, we will gain a good reputation. If we do not drink and stay away from the temptation of drugs, we will naturally have good health and wisdom.

By upholding the Five Precepts, we can eliminate our suffering, afflictions, and fear in this lifetime, and gain the freedom, peace, harmony, and joy of body and mind. In the future, we can escape from falling into the three lower realms, be reborn in the realms of humans and celestial beings, and even become a Buddha. Taking and upholding the Five Precepts is like planting seeds in the field of merits. Even if we do not seek it, we will still have many benefits and immeasurable merits.

UPHOLDING THE FIVE PRECEPTS

When we take and uphold the precepts, we take and uphold them unto the end of our bodily form; we do not uphold them only for a day. We can take all five precepts at one time, or take only those that we can uphold. The *Treatise on the Perfection of Great Wisdom* says, "There are Five Precepts. They begin with not killing and end with not taking intoxicants. If one precept is taken, it is called 'one unit.' If two or three precepts are taken, it is known as a 'few units.' If four precepts are taken, it is known as 'most units.' If five precepts are taken, it is called 'full units.' Of these units, how many units you wish to take is based on your own conditions."

From this, we see that laypeople can choose which precepts are easier for them to take according to their situation. They can take one, two, three, or four precepts, diligently uphold them, and gradually reach the state where they can uphold all five. In the future, they may also take the Eight Precepts of Purification or the Bodhisattva Precepts for the Laity. Through this kind of practice, they will naturally be reborn in the upper realms, be able reach the supreme states of cultivation, and finally attain Buddhahood.

Chapter Thirteen

FOLLOWING THE NOBLE EIGHTFOLD PATH

Suffering is the reality of life. How to attain ultimate liberation from this suffering is the purpose of learning Buddhism. When the Buddha first attained enlightenment, he taught eight methods for cultivating the way towards enlightenment in order to liberate all sentient beings from affliction and suffering. It is called the "Noble Eightfold Path."

Noble refers to breaking away from that which is evil and wrong. *Path* means, "being able to flow," and refers to flowing unobstructed to the state of nirvana. By following this Noble Eightfold Path, sentient beings can forever cut off their afflictions, suffering, and the causes of suffering, and attain the state of the sages–nirvana. Therefore, this path is called the eightfold path of the sages. The Noble Eightfold Path is like a boat that can carry sentient beings from the shore of ignorance to the shore of enlightenment, so it is also known as the boat of eight Dharma methods.

To put it simply, the Noble Eightfold Path is the Dharma method for cultivating the Way to Buddhahood. It is the way to be free from defilement and suffering. It is the right path of cultivation for Buddhist practitioners. When we follow and practice the Noble Eightfold Path, we can accomplish the ultimate goal of Buddhism. For this reason, we, as Buddhist practitioners, should understand the meaning of the Noble Eightfold Path.

THE NOBLE EIGHTFOLD PATH

The Noble Eightfold Path is what the Buddha taught after he attained enlightenment in the First Turning of the Dharma Wheel. From then on until he entered *parinirvana*, he also taught the four applications of mindfulness, the four right efforts, the four bases of spiritual power, the five faculties, the five powers, and the seven limbs of enlightenment. In total, they make up the thirty-seven practices leading to enlightenment, and are the teachings of the Fourth Noble Truth, (the path leading to the cessation of suffering). Of the thirty-seven practices leading to enlightenment, the Noble Eightfold Path best represents the Dharma method of cultivation in Buddhism. For this reason, we use the Noble Eightfold Path as the main discourse on the path leading to the cessation of suffering. The Noble Eightfold Path is: Right View, Right Thought, Right Speech, Right Action, Right Livelihood, Right Effort, Right Mindfulness, and Right Concentration.

Right View. "Right View" is having right concepts and right ideas. One concept can change a person's life. The object of learning Buddhism and of cultivating ourselves is to correct mistakes and bad habitual tendencies. This is why having the right views is so important. In the Buddhist sutras, there are many interpretations and explanations of Right View. According to the *Lion's Roar of Queen Srimala Sutra*, the views that are not deluded or confused are called Right View. The *Flower Ornament Sutra* says that when Right View becomes stronger, we will be far away from delusion. According to the *Treatise on the Perfection of Great Wisdom*, Right View is wisdom. The *Introduction to the Stages of Entering the Dharma Realm* says that cultivating the sixteen aspects of the Four Noble Truths and clearly seeing them is Right View.

In summary, Right View is the observation that leads us away from delusions and wrong views. It is the wisdom that truly comprehends cause and effect. It is the right understanding that results from contemplating phenomena through the Three Dharma Seals, the Four Noble Truths, and the Twelve Links of Dependent Origination. Looking at it from a broader perspective, we can see that all truths of Buddhism are considered Right View.

Right Thought. "Right Thought" is also known as right determination, right differentiation, right awareness, or right intention. The *Commentary on the Stages of Yogacara Practitioners* says, "When Right View is strengthened, thought without anger and harmfulness arises; this is Right Thought." Therefore, Right Thought is also not being greedy, not being angry, and not being ignorant; is far away from evil, delusion, greed, and desire; is contemplating and distinguishing with truth and wisdom.

The three poisons of greed, anger, and ignorance shackle us relentlessly, keeping us from seeking the Way. At any moment, these three poisons occupy our mind and pollute our pure original nature. If we wish to leave behind these three poisons, we must be firm in our resolve; we must always contemplate on the right Dharma; and we must possess the mind of gentleness, compassion, purity, and no anger. When our thoughts are in accord with the right Dharma at every moment, then we can eliminate the three poisons and enter the Way to Buddhahood.

Right Speech. "Right Speech" is wholesome verbal karma, and also refers to four of the ten wholesome conducts: not lying, not being double-tongued, not speaking harsh words, and not using flattery. It is removed from all careless, slanderous, arrogant, scolding, insulting, mean, flattering, and untrue words. This is why Right Speech is known as right words and true words. They must be words that are in accordance with the truth, so they are called "words that follow the truth." When the Buddha discoursed the Dharma, his words were all true, immutable, and undeceptive; this is Right Speech. There are four kinds of Right Speech:

1. Words of truth. These are words that are true, honest, and not duplicitous.
2. Words of compassion. These are words that are kind, soft, and give others confidence.
3. Words of praise. These are words that encourage others and bring them joy.
4. Words that benefit others. These are words that help and benefit others.

Right Action. "Right Action" is behavior that is right and in accord with the truth. It is wholesome bodily karma, which includes three of the ten wholesome conducts: not killing, not stealing, and not engaging in sexual misconduct. However, following this is just passively not committing unwholesome karma. The active meaning of Right Action is to protect life, be compassionate, and give charity.

Furthermore, the *Commentary on the Stages of Yogacara Practitioners* says, "In our lives, or in the pursuit of daily necessities, whether we are walking, staying, sitting, or reclining, if we can perform them with Right Thought, this is called Right Action." In other words, having a disciplined lifestyle is Right Action. For example, proper sleeping habits, diet, exercise, rest, and work habits, will not only improve our health and efficiency, but are also the main elements for a happy family and a peaceful society.

Right Livelihood. "Right Livelihood" refers to the right occupation and right way to make a living. According to the *Commentary on the Stages of Yogacara Practitioners*, "Following the Dharma in our pursuit of clothing, food, and other items, or staying away from all the ways of living that give rise to unwholesomeness, is Right Livelihood." Having a moral profession in life is extremely important because most unwholesomeness comes from doing things that harm others and ourselves. Working in a gambling house or a brothel, dealing drugs or arms, are all not examples of Right Livelihood because they involve killing, stealing, lying, engaging in sexual misconduct, and selling intoxicants.

Right Effort. "Right Effort" is also known as right diligence, right skillful means, true Dharma method, and true management. It means that we should move in the direction of Truth with courage and diligence. The sutras say, "If laypeople are lazy, they lose the benefits of the mundane world. If monastics are indolent, they lose the treasures of the Dharma." According to the *Sutra of the Right Mindfulness on the Dharma*, indolence is the root of all evil ways; it is the seed of the cycle of birth and death; it gives rise to all affliction and suffering in the world. If we wish to break the cycle of birth and death, we should be diligent and abandon indolence.

Diligence is not disorderly and does not retreat. It strives to do good and strives to sever evil. The *Treatise on the Perfection of Great Wisdom* says that we should take the four right efforts as the goal in our cultivation of diligence. The four right efforts are: to eliminate the unwholesomeness that has already been produced, to not produce unwholesomeness that has not yet been produced, to give rise to wholesomeness that has not yet been produced, and to increase the wholesomeness that has already been produced.

Right Mindfulness. "Right Mindfulness" is also known as true contemplation. It is a thought of purity and mindfulness. It does not give rise to unwholesomeness thoughts. It is contemplating the right Path. The *Sutra of the Teachings Bequeathed by the Buddha* says, "If we build a strong foundation of mindfulness, although we are surrounded by thieves of the five desires, we will not be harmed. It is like wearing armor into a battle and fearing nothing." This is why Buddhist practitioners should not pay any attention to gossip, desire, gain or loss, winning or losing, money or fame, and should always be mindful of Right Thought. There are four applications of Right Mindfulness. They are:

1. To contemplate that the body is impure. Attachments and delusions arise because most people are attached to the body, especially to its beauty and health. In fact, our bodies are filled with urine, excrement, mucus, saliva, and other waste products. We can say that it is where all waste products accumulate. The Buddha taught us to contemplate on the impurity of the body to eliminate our attachment to the body, so that we could cultivate ourselves through this body, and attain the eternal Dharmabody.

2. To contemplate that feelings are the origin of suffering. The feelings of pain and happiness in the mundane world all result in suffering. It is because life is filled with different kinds of

suffering such as birth, aging, sickness, and death. Even when we have happiness, due to the impermanence of all phenomena in the world, our happiness will eventually come to an end. Therefore, we should realize that feelings lead to suffering.

3. To contemplate that thoughts are impermanent. Our thoughts are changing at every second and every minute. Suddenly, they are in heaven; then, they are in hell. Sometimes, they are good; sometimes, they are bad. Sometimes, they arise; sometimes, they cease. For this reason, the Buddha said that we should contemplate on the impermanence of thoughts.

4. To contemplate that all phenomena have no substantial existence. The *Diamond Sutra* says, "All conditioned dharmas are like dreams, illusions, bubbles, and shadows. They are also like dewdrops and lightning. We should contemplate this." All phenomena in the world will eventually decay and extinguish; nothing in this world has a substantial existence. If we know how to contemplate on the fact that all phenomena have no substantial existence, we can find our Dharma nature amidst the five desires.

By always being mindful of impermanence, suffering, and no-self, we will not be attached to worldly advantages, and can bravery walk towards the Way.

Right concentration. "Right concentration" is using right *samadhi* to focus the mind and settle the distracted body so we can better cultivate ourselves. True *samadhi* is not merely a matter of sitting in meditation; it is also developing and exploring our inner capacity. Right Concentration should bring us good health. It should help us focus on single-mindedness and attain peace. It should clarify the mind and lead us from ignorance to the state of awakening. Ultimately, cultivating Right Concentration will reveal our Buddha nature to us and allow us to discover our true self.

THE IMPORTANCE OF THE NOBLE EIGHTFOLD PATH

The *Commentary on Abhidharma* says, "Right View gives rise to Right Thought; Right Thought leads to Right Speech; Right Speech leads to Right Action; Right Action initiates Right Livelihood; Right Livelihood initiates Right Effort; Right Effort then gives rise to Right Mindfulness; and Right Mindfulness can give rise to Right Concentration." If people have Right View, they will be able to have Right Thought and determine what is right or wrong, good or bad, and true or false. They will then perform Right Action of body, speech, and mind, and move in the right direction with Right Effort. They will also develop Right Mindfulness and abide in Right Concentration. We should realize that the Noble Eightfold Path is a unified whole. For any one of them to be fulfilled, it must be accompanied by the other seven elements.

Right View is the first step in the Noble Eightfold Path. Right View is bright wisdom and the teacher of cultivation. Buddhist practitioners must have Right View before they can see the truth of the universe. The *Connected Discourses of the Buddha* says, "If one has a strong foundation of Right View in the mundane world, although they will be reborn a thousand times, they will never fall into the three lower realms." From this, we can see the significance of Right View, and understand the importance of the Noble Eightfold Path without having to say a single word.

HOW TO PRACTICE THE NOBLE EIGHTFOLD PATH

The Dharma is not a theory, and we cannot just understand it from a philosophical point of view. This is especially true of the Noble Eightfold Path, which gives us guidance in our lives. For this reason, we need to practice and actualize it each and every day. When we do not change our belief in Buddhism in spite of how difficult it is to practice Buddhism, this is Right View. When our every thought is in accordance with the Dharma, this is Right Thought. When we speak with kind and compassionate words, giving others joy, hope, and confidence, this is Right Speech. When our actions are in accordance with morality; when we do not harm others just to satisfy our own desires; when we actively come to the aid of those in need of assistance; when we willingly give charity; when we strive to do good deeds and prevent evil; when we calmly use our wisdom to solve our problems in any kind of situation, these are all ways to practice the Noble Eightfold Path in our daily lives.

Chapter Fourteen

BECOMING A BODHISATTVA

In Mahayana Buddhism, the bodhisattvas are great practitioners who are walking on the path toward Buddhahood by benefiting all sentient beings as well as themselves. The path of the bodhisattva is a long, selfless journey through countless *kalpa*s that requires diligent cultivation of patience, compassion, mindfulness, and wisdom. Full of compassion for others, bodhisattvas make the great vow to liberate sentient beings from suffering and help them toward enlightenment.

The word "bodhisattva" is derived from two Sanskrit words: *bodhi* and *sattva*. *Bodhi* means "to enlighten" and *sattva* means "sentient beings." *Bodhisattva* means an "enlightening being" or a "sentient being who is seeking enlightenment." The term also refers to the practitioner who is seeking *bodhi*, helps others liberate themselves, cultivates various *paramitas*, and eventually will attain Buddhahood. Bodhisattvas are beings who accomplish the perfect practices of benefiting self and others, and bravely seek enlightenment.

THE WAY OF LIBERATING SENTIENT BEINGS

All bodhisattvas must make the vow to help all sentient beings and liberate them from suffering. There are two different ways they can fulfill their vows:

1. First liberate self, then liberate others. If one does not attain liberation first, how can one liberate others? When someone is drowning and we do not know how to swim ourselves, how can we save him? Therefore, before helping and liberating others, a bodhisattva must be liberated from *samsara* and must reach the state without affliction and suffering.

2. First liberate others before attaining self-liberation. This is

precisely the bodhisattva vow. A bodhisattva learns all Dharmas from sentient beings. If a bodhisattva cultivates the path away from sentient beings, then he can no longer be called a bodhisattva. When bodhisattvas completely liberate all sentient beings, that is when they complete the bodhisattva path.

Regardless of the approach we take, when we make a Mahayana vow to seek the Way, helping and liberating sentient beings becomes our primary responsibility. This is why we say, "Teaching Dharma is my duty; benefiting sentient beings is my mission."

THE MIND OF THE BODHISATTVA

The mind of the bodhisattva requires the mind of *bodhi*, the mind of great compassion, and the mind of skillful means. Master Taixu (1889-1947) said that the mind of *bodhi* is the cause, the mind of great compassion is the root, and the mind of skillful means is the ultimate truth. In Mahayana Buddhism, when practitioners are on the bodhisattva path, they must cultivate this kind of mind.

The mind of *bodhi* is the mind that seeks the attainment of Buddhahood. The Way to Buddhahood requires countless *kalpas* of cultivation before it can be attained. If we do not give rise to the supreme *bodhi* mind, how can we bear such long-term challenges?

The sutras say that if one more person in the world initiates the *bodhi* mind, there will be one more seed of enlightenment. Practicing Buddhism without giving rise to the *bodhi* mind is like tilling the land without sowing seeds. If we do not sow any seeds, how can we have a harvest in the future? The *bodhi* mind is one that makes the great vow. To initiate the *bodhi* mind is to make the Four Universal Vows. These vows are:

1. Sentient beings are infinite, I vow to liberate them.
2. Afflictions are endless, I vow to eradicate them.
3. Dharmas are inexhaustible, I vow to study them.

4. Buddhahood is supreme, I vow to attain it.

According to the *Flower Ornament Sutra*, "When one loses the *bodhi* mind, even if he cultivates various good conducts, they are considered 'evil actions.'" When bodhisattvas lose the *bodhi* mind, they cannot benefit any sentient beings. Therefore, the *bodhi* mind is the root of all wisdom and the basis of practicing great compassion.

The mind of great compassion is the mind that willingly liberates sentient beings. When bodhisattvas wish to come to the aid of sentient beings, they must have the mind of "great loving-kindness and great compassion." This means that bodhisattvas use their great loving-kindness to bring others joy and apply their great compassion to help rid others of suffering. Bodhisattvas should treat the suffering and happiness of all sentient beings as their own.

When they liberate sentient beings, they do not seek repayment, but rather, see helping others as their responsibility. The sayings, "Only wish to be the beasts of burden for sentient beings" and "Only wish that all sentient beings can be liberated from suffering, not seeking peace and happiness for oneself," illustrate more clearly the selfless nature of the bodhisattva's vow. This is the true mind of great compassion.

The mind of skillful means is the mind of practicing the four means of embracing. Since sentient beings have different needs and capacities for comprehension, bodhisattvas must apply skillful means wisely and extensively to save sentient beings from suffering. When the Buddha observed the different capacities of sentient beings, he discoursed on 84,000 Dharma methods, which all became the Buddha's applications of skillful means. Of these means, the bodhisattvas apply the four means of embracing–give charity, speak kind words, benefit others, and cooperate with others–so that sentient beings can give rise to ultimate great happiness. This is the mind of skillful means.

THE CHARACTERISTICS OF THE BODHISATTVA

The bodhisattva's most unique characteristics are compassion and selflessness. Whenever bodhisattvas see sentient beings suffering, great compassion arises from deep within their mind, and they make the great vow to save sentient beings from suffering in the Three Realms. Therefore, compassion is the force that moves bodhisattvas to practice the Buddha Way of benefiting self and others.

The compassion that bodhisattvas have for sentient beings is like the love that parents have for their children. In order to fulfill any need, they will sacrifice even their own lives. The bodhisattvas' great loving-kindness and compassion look after every sentient being like the sun shines on every corner of the land. Bodhisattvas take compassion as the foundation and then, based on the needs of the sentient being, apply *prajna*-wisdom to liberate them.

The best representative of the bodhisattva in Chinese Buddhism is the Great Compassionate Avalokitesvara Bodhisattva (better known by the name Guanyin). With his incomparable compassion, he made twelve great vows to liberate all sentient beings in the *saha* world. The name, Avalokitesvara, literally means, "He Who Hears the Sounds of the World" or "Perceiver of the Sounds of the World." At any time and any place, he follows the cries of those seeking assistance and applies his supernatural powers and skillful means to manifest before sentient beings. So long as there are sentient beings who cry out for help, Avalokitesvara Bodhisattva will appear and respond. In accordance with the various needs of sentient beings, he manifests in thirty-two bodily forms wherever he is needed to relieve suffering and distress.

In the "Chapter of the Universal Gate" of the *Lotus Sutra*, the Buddha expounds on how Avalokitesvara Bodhisattva came to be known as "Perceiver of the Sounds of the World":

Aksayamatir Bodhisattva said to the Buddha, "World-Honored One, how does Avalokitesvara Bodhisattva come and go in this *saha* world? How does he speak the Dharma for the sake of sentient beings? How does he use the power of skillful means?"

The Buddha said to Aksayamatir Bodhisattva: "Good man, if there are sentient beings in a land who need someone in the form of a Buddha in order to be liberated, Avalokitesvara Bodhisattva immediately manifests as a Buddha and speaks the Dharma for them. If they need someone in the form of a *pratyeka-buddha* to be liberated, he immediately manifests as a *pratyeka-buddha* and speaks the Dharma for them. If they need a *sravaka* to be liberated, he immediately manifests as a *sravaka* and speaks the Dharma for them. If they need Maha Brahma to be liberated, he immediately manifests as Maha Brahma and speaks the Dharma for them. If they need *Sakra* to be liberated, he immediately manifests as *Sakra* and speaks the Dharma for them. If they need to King Mahesvara to be liberated, he immediately manifests as King Mahesvara and speaks the Dharma for them. If they need a great general of heaven to be liberated, he immediately manifests as a great general of heaven and speaks the Dharma for them. If they need *Vaisravana* to be liberated, he immediately manifests as *Vaisravana* and speaks the Dharma for them. If they need a king to be liberated, he immediately manifests as a king and speaks the Dharma for them. If they need an elder to be liberated, he immediately manifests as an elder and speaks the Dharma for them. If they need a layperson to be liberated, he immediately manifests as a layperson and speaks the Dharma for them. If they need a prime minister to be liberated, he immediately manifests as a prime minister and speaks the Dharma for them. If they need a brahman to be liberated, he immediately manifests as a brahman and speaks the Dharma for them. If they need a *bhiksu*, a *bhiksuni*, an *upasaka*, or an *upasika* to be liberated, he immediately manifests as a *bhiksu*, a *bhiksuni*, an *upasaka*, or an *upasika* and speaks the Dharma for them. If they need the wife of an elder, of a layperson, a prime minister, or a brahman to be liberated, he immediately manifests as those wives and speaks the Dharma for them. If they need a young boy or a young girl to be liberated, he immediately manifests as a young boy or a young girl and speaks the Dharma for them. If they need a celestial being, a dragon, a *yaksa*, a *gandharva*, an *asura*, a *garunda*, a *kimnara*, a *mahoraga*, a human or nonhuman being to be liberated, he immediately manifests as all of these and speaks the Dharma for them. If they need a vajra deva to be liberated, he immediately manifests as a vajra deva and speaks the Dharma for them.

"Aksayamatir Bodhisattva, this Avalokitesvara Bodhisattva has accomplished such merits and virtues by assuming different forms and traveling to various lands to liberate sentient beings. For this reason, you all should wholeheartedly make offerings to Avalokitesvara Bodhisattva. This Avalokitesvara Bodhisattva Mahasattva can, amidst terror and crisis, bestow fearlessness. That is why this *saha* world calls him the 'Bestower of Fearlessness.'"

To Mahayana Buddhists, Avalokitesvara Bodhisattva is widely considered to be the very embodiment of the Buddha's compassion. His deep cultivation is precisely the characteristic of the bodhisattva's compassion and selflessness.

THE PRACTICE OF THE BODHISATTVA PATH

Buddhism is a religion that emphasizes practice, but it is also a philosophy with the ethical characteristics. Since the *Buddhist Canon* describes many profound doctrines with specific viewpoints about the truth of the universe, it is considered a philosophy. However, because Buddhism places great importance on

the application of morality and ethics to life, we say that it is a religion. In fact, the Buddha was himself regarded as the role model
for the fulfillment of moral practice. After the Buddha attained
enlightenment, he repeatedly stressed, "Do no evil; do good deeds.
Purify one's mind; this is all Buddhism," with the hope that all sentient beings could purify themselves by cultivating moral conduct.

The practice of the bodhisattva path is just like the process
of learning; it goes step by step. From the state of the ordinary person who has afflictions to the state of the awakening bodhisattva
who has cut off all defilements, there are definite stages of cultivation. In order to reach sagehood, each stage requires the fulfillment of the thirty-seven practices leading to enlightenment, the
four means of embracing, and the six perfections.

The thirty-seven practices leading to enlightenment are the
four applications of mindfulness, the four right efforts, the four
bases of spiritual power, the five faculties, the five powers, the
seven limbs of enlightenment, and the Noble Eightfold Path. These
methods are the resources that can help us cut off unwholesome
deeds, develop wholesome conduct, eliminate ignorance, and enter
the *bodhi* path. For these reasons, the practitioners on the bodhisattva path should diligently cultivate the thirty-seven practices
to achieve enlightenment.

On the bodhisattva path, the most important Dharma
method is the six perfections, also known as the six *paramitas*.
The literal meaning of *paramita* is "having reached the other
shore," or having accomplished the goal of enlightenment. The six
perfections liberate the deluded and lead them to enlightenment,
liberate the evil and put them on the right path, liberate the suffering and give them happiness, and liberate all sentient beings from
this shore of affliction and ferry them across to the other shore of
liberation. The six perfections constitute the six forms of practice
that bodhisattvas must realize in order to accomplish Buddhahood.
They are: the perfection of giving charity, the perfection of upholding the precepts, the perfection of patience, the perfection of diligence, the perfection of meditation, and the perfection of *prajna*-
wisdom.

1. The perfection of giving charity is the generous mind of giving charity without attachment to form. All forms of giving should be carried out without clinging to what has been given, who is doing the giving, and who is receiving the gift. This is the bodhisattvas' way of giving charity.

2. The perfection of upholding the precepts is the non-violating mind of respecting sentient beings. Observing the Buddhist precepts, acting in accordance with right Dharma, and practicing the path of benefiting sentient beings is the bodhisattvas' way of upholding the precepts.

3. The perfection of patience is the equanimous mind that endures what is difficult to endure. In order to learn all Dharmas, one should practice the Dharma method of patience by being tolerant in situations of persecution, by being accepting in circumstances of adversity, and by contemplating all truths. When one is able to do what is difficult to do and endure what is difficult to endure without retreating in fear, this is the bodhisattvas' way of practicing patience.

4. The perfection of diligence is the fearless mind that refrains from evil and practices good deeds. On the path of cultivation, bodhisattvas do not fear obstacles. They diligently practice courage, diligently practice wholesome Dharmas, and diligently practice bringing joy and benefiting others. They do not tire of teaching even the most obstinate of sentient beings, but instead apply their efforts ceaselessly.

5. The perfection of meditation is the non-differentiating mind of right mindfulness. Bodhisattvas apply their meditative concentration to settle themselves and others, and to demonstrate right mindfulness to all sentient beings.

6. The perfection of *prajna*-wisdom is the mind of great wisdom that is beyond the duality of emptiness and existence. Bodhisattvas skillfully apply their great wisdom to inspire in sentient beings what is right and good, and gradually liberate them from their suffering.

The spirit of the bodhisattvas' six perfections is altruistic, and the meaning is profound. A true practitioner of Buddhism must put them into practice, protect the Dharma, and allow the Dharma to spread throughout the universe; and with a sincere attitude, create a bright future that benefits our communities. When we can generate the same compassion and the same awakened mind as the bodhisattvas, and cultivate the six perfections to the benefit of self and others, then the pure land of Humanistic Buddhism will manifest before us.

GLOSSARY

Ananda: One of the ten great disciples of the Buddha. He is noted as the foremost in hearing and learning. After the Buddha entered *parinirvana*, Ananda is said to have compiled the sutras in Vaibhara Cave, which is located in Magadha, India, where the five hundred disciples of the Buddha assembled.

Avalokitesvara Bodhisattva: Literally, "He Who Hears the Sounds of the World" or "Perceiver of the Sounds of the World." In Mahayana Buddhism, Avalokitesvara is known as the Bodhisattva of Compassion. He can manifest himself in any form necessary to help any being. He is considered one of the great bodhisattvas in Mahayana Buddhism. In China, he is usually portrayed in female form and is known as "Guanyin."

Bhiksu: The male members of the Buddhist sangha, who have renounced household life and received full ordination.

Bhiksuni: The female members of the Buddhist sangha who have renounced household life and received full ordination.

Bodhi: It means enlightenment. In the state of enlightenment, one is awakened to the true nature of self; one is enlightened to one's own Buddha nature. Such a person has already eliminated all afflictions and delusions, and achieved *prajna*-wisdom.

Bodhi mind: *Sanskrit, bodhicitta.* The mind that seeks enlightenment.

Bodhisattva: Refers to one who is seeking the attainment of Buddhahood or liberation, and one who practices all perfections. Bodhisattvas remain in the world to help others achieve enlightenment. The concept of the bodhisattva is the defining feature of Mahayana Buddhism.

Bodhisattva path: Indicates the cultivation of the bodhisattvas in Mahayana Buddhism. The main philosophy of the bodhisattva path is to attain Buddhahood and liberate all sentient beings through the practice of the four means of embracing and the six perfections.

Brahmans: In ancient India, the highest of four castes. Traditionally, they were the teachers and interpreters of religious knowledge. They were also the priests who acted as intermediaries between god, the world, and humans. In ancient Indian society, they were the only group allowed to change and perform the rituals of worship.

Buddha: Literally, "enlightened one." When "the Buddha" is used, it usually refers to the historical Buddha, Sakyamuni Buddha.

Buddha nature: The inherent nature that exists in all beings. It is the capability to achieve Buddhahood.

Buddhahood: The attainment and expression that characterizes a Buddha. Buddhahood is the ultimate goal of all sentient beings.

Buddhism: Founded by Sakyamuni Buddha around 2,500 years ago. Its basic doctrines include the Three Dharma Seals, the Four Noble Truths, the Noble Eightfold Path, the Twelve Links of Dependent Origination, the six perfections, and the concepts of karma, impermanence, and emptiness. Its three main traditions are the Mahayana, Theravada, and Vajrayana. While Buddhism has been a popular religion in South, Central, and East Asia, it is currently gaining popularity in the West.

Cause and condition: Referring to the primary cause (causes) and the secondary causes (conditions). The seed out of which a plant or flower grows is a good illustration of a primary cause; the elements of soil, humidity, sunlight, and so forth, could be considered secondary causes.

Cause and effect: This is the most basic doctrine in Buddhism, which explains the formation of all relations and connections in the world. This law means that the arising of each and every phenomenon is due to its own causes and conditions, and the actual form, or appearance, of all phenomena is the effect.

Celestial beings: Eight groups of celestial beings, including *devas, nagas, yaksas, asuras, garudas, gandharvas, kinnaras,* and *mahoragas.* 1) *Devas*: gods who reside above the human realm and between the heavens. They are still unenlightened and therefore subject to the cycle of birth and death. 2) *Naga*s: serpents or dragons that are beneficial half-divine beings that climb into the heavens in spring and live deep in the earth in winter. 3) *Yaksas*: swift powerful ghosts that are usually harmful, but sometimes act as protectors of the Dharma. 4) *Asuras*: angry and contentious celestial beings who continually fight with the god Indra in Indian mythology. They are said to live at the bottom of the oceans surrounding Mt. Sumeru. 5) *Garudas*: celestial birds with strong large wings. 6) *Gandharvas*: celestial musicians associated with the court of the celestial monarch Indra. 7) *Kinnaras*: also known as kimnaras, they are also celestial musicians. They have a horse-like head with one horn and a human-like body. Males sing and females dance. 8) *Mahoragas*: beings shaped like boas or great snakes. These eight classes are all the parts of the retinue of Sakyamuni Buddha and of the Dharma protectors.

Chan: The Chinese transliteration of the Sanskrit term, *dhyana*; it refers to meditative concentration.

Chan School: One school of Chinese Buddhism. It was founded by Bodhidharma, emphasizes the cultivation of intrinsic wisdom, and teaches that enlightenment is clarifying the mind and seeing one's own true nature. Another major tenet of the Chan School is that the Dharma is wordlessly transmitted from mind to mind.

Dependent Origination: The central principle that phenomena do not come into existence independently but only as a result of causes and conditions; therefore, no phenomena possesses an independent self-nature. This concept is also referred to as interdependence. The twelve factors of dependent origination are: ignorance, karma, formation of consciousness, mind and body, the six senses, contact, feeling, craving, grasping, becoming, birth, and aging and death.

Dharma: When capitalized, it means: 1) the ultimate truth and 2) the teachings of the Buddha. When the Dharma is applied or practiced in life it is referred to as: 3) righteousness or virtues. When it appears with a lowercase "d": 4) anything that can be thought of, experienced, or named; close in meaning to "phenomena."

Dharma-body: *Sanskrit, Dharmakaya.* Refers to the true nature of a Buddha, and also to the absolute Dharma that the Buddha attained. It is also one of three bodies possessed by a Buddha.

Dharma realm: *Sanskrit, dharma-dhatu.* It indicates the notion of true nature that encompasses all phenomena. As a space or realm of dharmas, it is the uncaused and immutable totality in which all phenomena arise, abide, and extinguish.

Emptiness: A basic concept in Buddhism. It means that everything existing in the world is due to dependent origination and has no permanent self or substance.

Eighty noble qualities: Also known as "eighty accessory marks." The minor characteristics of Buddhas or bodhisattvas.

Five aggregates: Indicates form, feeling, perception, mental formation, and consciousness.

Five faculties: They are: 1) faith on the right path; 2) diligence on the right Dharmas; 3) remembering the right Dharmas without forgetting; 4) concentration, in which the mind is stable and without distractions; and 5) wisdom, to contemplate and see the nature of all Dharmas.

Five powers: They are: 1) when the power of faith increases, doubts can be eliminated; 2) when the power of diligence increases, the sloth of body and mind can be eliminated; 3) when the power of remembrance increases, unwholesome thoughts can be eliminated; 4) when the power of concentration increases, distractions can be eliminated and the state of *samadhi* can be attended; and 5) when the power of wisdom increases, delusions can be stopped and eliminated.

Five Precepts: The fundamental principles of conduct and discipline that were established by the Buddha for wholesome and harmonious living. They are: 1) do not kill; 2) do not steal; 3) do not lie; 4) do not engage in sexual misconduct; and 5) do not take intoxicants.

Four applications of mindfulness: They are mindfulness on the body, feelings, thoughts and phenomena (dharmas): 1) to contemplate that the body is impure; 2) to contemplate that feelings are the origin of suffering; 3) to contemplate that thoughts are impermanent, always arising then extinguishing; and 4) to contemplate that all phenomena have no substantial existence.

Four bases of spiritual power: They are: 1) the spiritual power of desire-to-do, which means that all Dharmas of cultivation can be fulfilled; 2) the spiritual power of diligence, which means that the mind can concentrate on cultivation without interruptions; 3) the spiritual power of remembering, which means that the mind does not forget; and 4) the spiritual power of contemplation, which means the mind contemplates all Dharmas.

Four heavenly kings: According to Buddhist cosmology, there are four mythical kings who live halfway down Mt. Sumeru. King Dhrtarastra is in the East; King Virudhaka is in the South; King Virupaksa is in the West; and King Dhanada (or Vaisravana) is in the North.

Four means of embracing: The four methods that bodhisattvas use to guide sentient beings to the path of liberation: 1) giving charity; 2) speaking kind words; 3) benefiting others; and 4) cooperating with others.

Four Noble Truths: A foundation and essential teaching of Buddhism that describes the presence of suffering, the cause of suffering, the path leading to the cessation of suffering, and the cessation of suffering.

Four Reliances: Four guidelines to keep Buddhists on the right path. They are: 1) rely on the Dharma, not on people; 2) rely on wisdom, not on knowledge; 3) rely on meaning, not on words; and 4) rely on definitive meaning, not on provisional meaning.

Four Right Efforts: They are: 1) to eliminate the unwholesomeness that has already been produced; 2) to not produce unwholesomeness that has not yet been produced; 3) to give rise to wholesomeness that has not yet been produced; and 4) to increase the wholesomeness that has already been produced.

Gongan: Also known in Japanese as *koan*. Literally "public notice" in Chinese that originally referred to a legal precedent. However, this became a term adopted by the Chan tradition to refer to a phrase, or question and answer exchange that points to an essential paradox. Contemplation of a *gongan* is aimed at transcending logical or conceptual assumptions in order to intuit the ultimate reality of emptiness.

Impermanence: One of the most basic truths taught by the Buddha. It is the concept that all conditioned dharmas, or phenomena, will arise, abide, change, and disappear due to causes and conditions.

Kalpa: The measuring unit of time in ancient India; a *kalpa* is an immense and inconceivable length of time. Buddhism adapts it to refer to the period of time between the creation and re-creation of the worlds.

Karma: This means "work, action, or deeds" and is related to the Law of Cause and Effect. All deeds, whether good or bad, produce effects. The effects may be experienced instantly, or they may not come into fruition for many years or even many lifetimes.

Mahayana: Mahayana, literally means "Great Vehicle." One of the two main traditions of Buddhism, Theravada being the other one. Mahayana Buddhism stresses that helping other sentient beings achieve enlightenment is as important as self-liberation.

Maitreya Bodhisattva: The future Buddha. It is said that he currently presides over Tusita Heaven, where he is expounding the Dharma to heavenly beings in the inner palace.

Nirvana: *Pali, nibbana.* The original meaning of this word is "extinguished, calmed, quieted, tamed, or dead." In Buddhism, it refers to the absolute extinction of individual existence, or of all afflictions and desires; it is the state of liberation, beyond birth and death. It is also the final goal in Buddhism.

No-self: A basic concept in Buddhism. It means that all phenomena and beings in the world have no real, permanent, and substantial self. Everything arises, abides, changes, and extinguishes based on the Law of Dependent Origination.

Noble Eightfold Path: Eight right ways leading to liberation. They are: 1) Right View; 2) Right Thought; 3) Right Speech; 4) Right Action; 5) Right Livelihood; 6) Right Effort; 7) Right Mindfulness; and 8) Right Concentration.

Parinirvana: A synonym for *nirvana*. It is the state of having completed all merits and perfections and eliminated all unwholesomeness. Usually, it is used to refer to the time when the Buddha physically passed away.

Period of Decling Dharma: The last period of the Dharma influence, which is divided into three periods. They are: 1) the Period of Right Dharma; 2) the Period of Semblance Dharma; and 3) the Period of Declining Dharma.

Prajna-wisdom: *Prajna*-wisdom is the highest form of wisdom. It is the wisdom of insight into the true nature of all phenomena.

Pratyeka-buddha: Refers to those who awaken to the Truth through their own efforts when they live in a time without a Buddha's presence.

Pure Land: Another term for a Buddha realm, which is established by the vows and cultivation of one who has achieved enlightenment.

Rahula: The son of Prince Siddhartha; one of the Buddha's ten great disciples. At a young age, he entered the Sangha and was instructed by Sariputra. He was considered foremost in inconspicuous practice.

Saha world: Literally, *saha* means endurance. It indicates the present world where we reside, which is full of suffering to be endured. The beings in this world endure suffering and afflictions due to their greed, anger, hatred, and ignorance.

Sakya clan: Refers to the tribe to which Sakyamuni Buddha belonged.

Sakyamuni Buddha: The historical founder of Buddhism. He was born the prince of Kapilavastu, son of King Suddhodana. At the age of twenty-nine, he left the royal palace and his family to search for the meaning of existence. At the age of thirty-five, he attained enlightenment under the *bodhi* tree. He then spent the next forty-five years expounding his teachings, which include the Four Noble Truths, the Noble Eightfold Path, the Law of Cause and Effect, and dependent origination. At the age of eighty, he entered the state of *parinirvana*.

Samadhi: Literally, "establish" or "make firm." It means concentration; a state in which the mind is concentrated in a one-pointed focus and all mental activities are calm. In *samadhi*, one is free from all distractions, thereby entering a state of inner serenity.

Samsara: Also known as the cycle of birth and death or transmigration. When sentient beings die, they are reborn into one of the six realms of existence. The cycle is continuous and endless due to the karmic result of one's deeds.

Sangha: Indicating the Buddhist community; in a broad sense it includes both monastics and laypeople. Specifically, it refers to the monastics.

Sentient beings: *Sanskrit, sattvas.* All beings with consciousness, including celestial beings, asuras, humans, animals, hungry ghosts, and hell beings. From the Mahayana view, all sentient beings inherently have Buddha nature and therefore possess the capacity to attain enlightenment.

Seven limbs of enlightenment: This refers to seven kinds of practices to develop enlightenment. They are: 1) mindfulness, 2) investigation of Dharmas, 3) diligence, 4) joyfulness, 5) ease of body and mind, 6) concentration, and 7) equanimity.

Six dusts: Indicating the six objects reflected by the six bases (sense-organs), which then produce the six consciousnesses.

Six perfections: Also known as the six *paramitas*. *Paramita* in Sanskrit means "having reached the other shore," "transcendent," "complete attainment," "perfection in," and "transcendental virtue." The six perfections are: 1) giving charity; 2) upholding precepts; 3) patience; 4) diligence; 5) meditation; and 6) *prajna*-wisdom.

Six organs: Refers to the eyes, ears, nose, tongue, body, and mind.

Six realms: Or the six realms of existence, indicating the realms of heaven, human, *asura*, animals, hungry ghost, and hell.

Sravaka: Literally, the word *sravaka* means hearer, and it refers to one who has attained enlightenment after listening to the Buddha's teachings.

Suchness: A term for the true nature of all things; the pure, original essence of all phenomena, which is called *tathata* or *bhuta-tathata*.

Suddhodana: The father of Prince Siddhartha, the ruler of Kapilavastu, and the eldest son of Simhahanu. His wife was Queen Maya, but he later married Mahapajapati, the queen's sister following her death.

Supernatural power: That which is beyond or above the natural, or cannot be controlled by natural law. In Buddhism, there are six kinds of supernatural powers: the power of psychic traveling, clairaudience (deva-ear), clairvoyance (deva-eye), mental telepathy, knowledge of past and future, and ending contamination.

Tathagata: One of the ten epithets of Buddha, literally translated as "Thus-Come One," meaning the one who has attained full realization of suchness; i.e. the one with the absolute, so that he neither comes from anywhere nor goes anywhere.

Ten wholesome conducts: The ten wholesome actions are: no killing, no stealing, no sexual misconduct, no lying, no duplicity, no harsh words, no flattery, no greed, no anger, and no ignorance.

The Way: Refers to the path leading to liberation taught by the Buddha.

Thirty-seven practices leading to enlightenment: Also known as thirty-seven wings of enlightenment. They are the four applications of mindfulness, the four right efforts, the four bases of spiritual power, the five faculties, the five powers, the seven limbs of enlightenment, and the Noble Eightfold Path.

Thirty-two marks of excellence: Also known as "the thirty-two excellent marks of the Buddha." They are the remarkable physical characteristics possessed by a Buddha; the symbols of qualities attained at the highest level of cultivation are: 1) the soles of the feet are flat, 2) the symbol of a wheel on the soles of the feet and on two hands, 3) long, slender fingers, 4) broad heels, 5) curved toes and fingers, 6) soft and smooth hands and feet, 7) the top of the feet are rounded, 8) a lower body like that of an antelope, 9) arms reaching to the knees, 10) a virile member without narrowing in the foreskin, 11) a powerful body, 12) a hairy body, 13) thick, curly hair, 14) a golden-hued body, 15) a body that gives off rays ten feet in every direction, 16) soft skin, 17) rounded hands, shoulders, and head, 18) well-formed shoulders, 19) an upper body like that of a lion, 20) an erect body, 21) powerful and muscular shoulders, 22) forty teeth, 23) even teeth, 24) white teeth, 25) cheeks like that of a lion, 26) an ability to appreciate the wonderful taste of all foods, 27) a broad, long tongue, 28) a voice like that of a Brahma, 29) clear and blue eyes, 30) eyelashes like that of a bull, 31) a cone-shaped elevation on the crown of the head, and 32) a lock of hair between the eyebrows.

Three Dharma Seals: Also known as the Three Marks of Existence. They are as follows: 1) all phenomena are impermanent; 2) all phenomena do not have a substantial self; and 3) nirvana is perfect tranquility.

Three poisons: Greed, anger, and ignorance.

Three Realms: The realms where sentient beings reside and transmigrate: 1) the realm of sense-desires; 2) the realm of form; and 3) the realm of formlessness.

Three Studies: Includes precepts, meditative concentration, and wisdom. Precepts can prevent one from the unwholesomeness of body, speech, and mind. Concentration can help one eliminate distracting thoughts with a singly focused mind, see the true nature, and attain the path. Wisdom can enable one to reveal the true nature, eliminate all afflictions, and see the Truth.

Tripitaka: The *Buddhist Canon* known as "Three Baskets." It is divided into three categories: the sutras (teachings of the Buddha), the *vinayas* (precepts and rules), and the *abhidharma* (commentaries on the Buddha's teachings).

Triple Gem: Indicating the Buddha, the Dharma, and the Sangha, and also called the Triple Jewel, or the Three Jewels. The Buddha is the fully awakened or enlightened one; the Dharma is the teachings imparted by the Buddha; and the Sangha indicates the community of monastic members.

Upasaka: A layman; a male follower of Buddhism who does not renounce the household life and enter a monastery but who still strives to live a spiritually-cultivated life and upholds the teachings and precepts.

Upasika: A female follower of Buddhism who practices the teachings of the Buddha and upholds the precepts.

Without Outflow: Outflows is called *asrava* in Sanskrit and *youlou* in Chinese. Literally, *lou* means leaking, and in Buddhism it represents afflictions. The state of "without outflows" (*Sanskrit, anasrava; Chinese, wulou*) refers to the state of liberation. Sometimes "without outflows" refers to those dharmas free from afflictions and leading to liberation.

World-Honored One: One of ten epithets of a Buddha. Traced back to the original Sanskrit term, *loka-natha* refers to the lord of the worlds, or *loka-jyestha* means the most venerable of the world. Today, it is usually translated as "the World-Honored One."

Notes